PRACTICAL
PATCHWORK
& APPLIQUE
TECHNIQUES

PRACTICAL
PATCHWORK
& APPLIQUE
TECHNIQUES

EDITED BY GAIL LAWTHER

TIGER BOOKS INTERNATIONAL
LONDON

A QUINTET BOOK

This edition first published in 1991 by
Tiger Books International PLC
London

Copyright © 1991 Quintet Publishing Limited

ISBN 1-85501-179-4

This book was designed and produced by
Quintet Publishing Limited
6 Blundell Street
London N7 9BH

Designer: Miranda Snow
Project Editor: Gail Lawther
Editor: Laura Sandelson

Typeset in Great Britain by
Typestyles, Essex
Manufactured in Singapore by
Chroma Graphics (Overseas) PTE. LTD.
Printed in Spain by
Gráficas Estella, S.A. Navarra.

The material in this publication previously
appeared in *Needlework School, Complete Guide
to Needlework, Sewing Techniques, Quilts: How to
Design and Make Your Own* and *The Quilting,
Patchwork and Appliqué Project Book.*

CONTENTS

INTRODUCTION

Both patchwork and appliqué have their roots in thrift. In days when fabrics were more expensive and harder to obtain than they are now, it made sense to hoard scraps of fabric left over after cutting out garments or furnishings and to build the scraps up into a coverlet or rug. Or, of course, if a dress or sheet had worn out in places the good bits of fabric could be re-used in a patchwork quilt. Appliqué was similarly practical; if a garment or a cushion had been worn through or been torn in one area, a shaped patch could be stiched over the damaged area and the item could still be used. In countries where clothes and fabrics are still hard to obtain, both techniques are still used to get the longest possible life out of a piece of precious fabric.

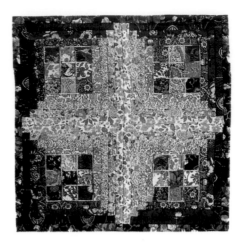

In the western world both crafts declined as mass-produced clothing and furnishings became cheap and readily available, and it seemed as though patchwork and appliqué, along with other crafts such as lacemaking and embroidery, were dying out. But during the 1960s and 1970s people began to rediscover the satisfaction and creativity of many traditional crafts, and patchwork and appliqué were two that benefited from a revival of interest. This book will teach you the fundamental principles of each technique so that you can join the other needleworkers who are using traditional and modern designs to produce pieces of work that are fulfilling to stitch and beautiful to look at.

The first section of the book briefly introduces the materials and equipment that you will need to produce good patchwork and appliqué pieces. You will probably have most of this equipment at home, but you might want to invest in a few specialised items such as a pair of compasses for drawing patchwork templates, or an embroidery frame so that you can keep your fabric taut as you stitch appliqué motifs.

The second section takes you through the basic principles and techniques of patchwork, explaining the different types and patterns and how you can produce them, and showing many examples of finished patchwork pieces. The techniques cover English patchwork (using paper templates), American patchwork, and applied patchwork in which the fabric patches are stitched in different arrangements onto a backing fabric. The section finishes with some inspirational examples of contemporary patchwork, to show you just how creative and versatile this craft can be.

Section three deals with appliqué, beginning with the basic stitching methods then working through the many different appliqué techniques, using everything from sheer nets through to patches cut from patterned fabrics. This section too, finishes with some inspirational examples of modern appliqué work.

The final section of the book shows you different ways in which you can finish off your project, from adding embroidery to creating

special borders and bindings. There are several pages on quilting your finished piece — stitching it to a padded backing so that the stitching forms an extra dimension to your design. Finally, there are hints on mounting your finished projects so that they can be displayed.

So, if you can use a needle and thread, this book will teach you the basic skills you need to produce your own patchwork and appliqué projects. Whether you're designing your own pattern or following one from the book, you'll be encouraged by how easy it is to produce attractive results, right from your first attempts.

Chapter One

MATERIALS & EQUIPMENT

GENERAL DRAWING EQUIPMENT

For designing, marking fabrics and making templates you will need rulers (both plastic and metal), and a set square (right-angle triangle), a protractor, a pair of compasses and a range of coloured crayons, lead pencils and chalk pencils — a set of felt pens is also useful for making your own designs. There are various proprietary 'magic' markers available for transferring designs to fabric. These are particularly useful if you are quilting your finished patchwork or appliqué, when it is crucial to have a lightly marked design that does not permanently stain the fabric. You will also need a sharp craft knife.

Paper

Use cartridge (sketching) paper, shelf paper or artist's detail paper for planning designs, where several sheets can be taped together for working out very large patterns.

Graph paper is recommended for planning scaled patchwork designs and borders and for shaping templates. Isometric graph paper is extremely helpful for constructing certain patchwork templates such as the hexagon and equilateral triangle.

You will need tracing paper or tissue paper for transferring designs. Dressmaker's carbon paper is also used for transferring designs to fabric and gives a fairly long-lasting mark. It is available in several colours including red, yellow, blue, black and white. Choose the colour nearest to your background fabric or thread, and also white, or other light colours, to show up on dark fabrics.

Notepaper is the ideal weight for backing papers used with hand-sewn cotton or silk patchwork. Thicker fabrics, however, may need slightly heavier papers. The paper should be sufficiently firm for its edges to be felt through the folds of the fabric.

Card, Abrasive Paper and Acetate

Templates for patchwork and appliqué can be made from these materials to suit your own designs; thin ticket card (thin cardboard) is generally recommended. Abrasive paper (a fine sandpaper, for example) is especially good for gripping the fabric but, with repeated use, it has the disadvantage of wearing out at the edges. Both card and abrasive paper templates can be strengthened with tape, and duplicates can always be made. For very large projects, where the templates have to withstand repeated use, it is a good idea to use a more durable material such as acetate; this is available from art supply shops.

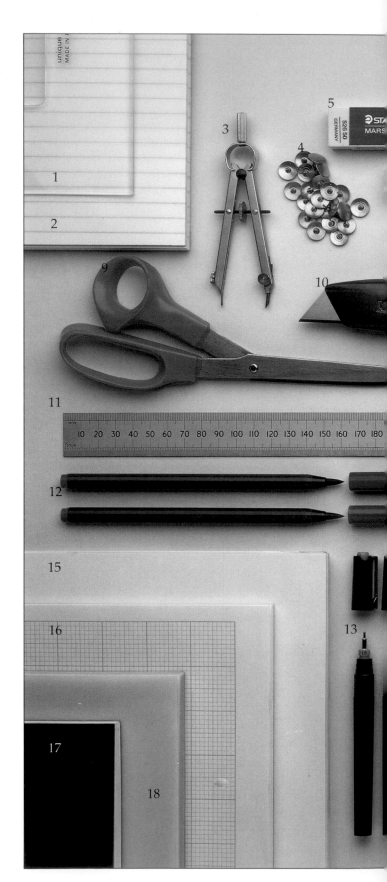

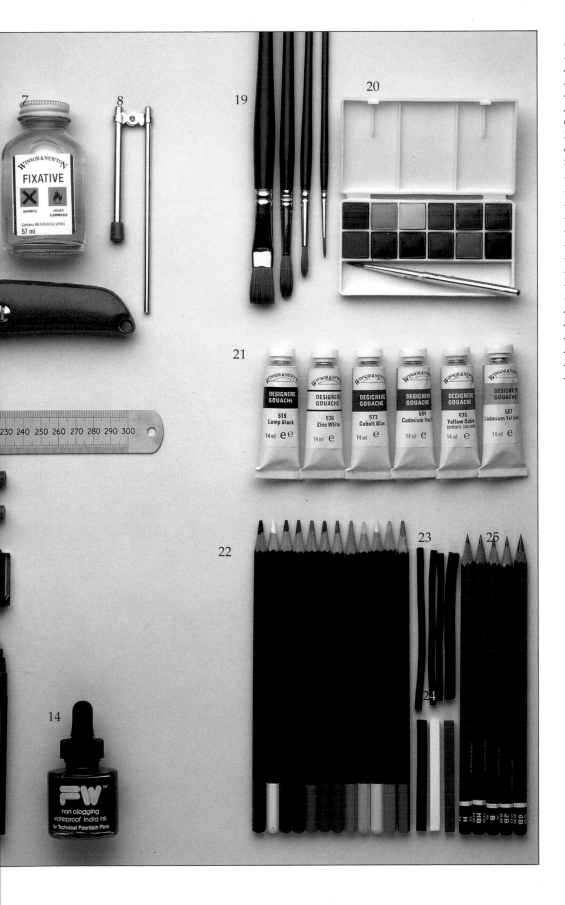

LEFT
1 Set square
2 Notebook
3 Compasses
4 Drawing pins
5 Plastic eraser
6 Pencil sharpener
7 Fixative
8 Spray diffuser
9 Shears
10 Craft knife
11 Steel rule
12 Felt-tip markers
13 Technical pens
14 Non-clogging ink
15 Cartridge paper
16 Squared paper
17 Tracing paper
18 Sketch book
19 Brushes
20 Watercolours
21 Gouaches
22 Conté crayons
23 Charcoal
24 Chalks
25 Pencils

GENERAL SEWING EQUIPMENT

Very little specialised sewing equipment is needed for patchwork and appliqué; you will probably find that you have most of it already in your sewing workbox. A good selection of pins is needed including fine lace pins for delicate fabrics, dressmaker's stainless pins for general use, and glass-headed pins for pinning together several thicknesses. You will also need a measuring tape and a dressmaker's tracing wheel for transferring designs, using the carbon paper method. Many craftworkers who do not use a thimble for ordinary hand sewing will find that one is very useful for patchwork.

Needles

Using the best needle for the task in hand will not only give the best results, it will save a good deal of frustration! If you use a needle that is too large the thread will keep slipping out of it, and the needle may make unsightly marks on the fabric. If your needle is too small, it will be difficult to thread it properly and difficult to pull it through the fabric. For ordinary hand-sewn patchwork and appliqué the best needles are sharps and crewels; keep a selection of different sizes so that you can choose the best one for each sewing project.

Threads

It is important to choose the thread that will give the best results for your particular needs. Either match the thread to the fabric being used, silk thread for silk fabric, for example, or in patchwork or quilting, use quilting thread. Quilting thread is smoother and stronger than ordinary cotton threads and comes in a fairly good selection of colours. Otherwise, No. 50 or No. 60 heavy duty mercerized cotton is an excellent alternative. Cotton/polyester threads and synthetic threads tend to knot and fray and are not generally recommended for hand sewing. However, as with other hand-sewing threads, they can be drawn through a block of beeswax which should strengthen them and prevent twisting.

Scissors

For accurate cutting, use sharp dressmaker's shears, and keep them for cutting only fabrics so as not to blunt the blades. For snipping into corners and curves, when doing padded quilting, and for cutting threads, small embroidery scissors are good. General purpose scissors are needed for cutting paper and card.

LEFT A well-stocked sewing workbox will have most of the items necessary for patchwork and appliqué: sharp scissors, a tape measure, pins, needles in various sizes, and different kinds of threads.

OTHER USEFUL EQUIPMENT

As well as drawing and sewing equipment, there are several other items that you will need for your patchwork and appliqué projects. Labour-saving devices such as frames and a sewing machine will make your life easier when you are working on large projects, and a good selection of fabric scraps will give you plenty of choice when you are looking for fabrics that match or contrast attractively.

Frames

Rectangular, or slate, frames and large embroidery or quilting hoops are ideal for hand-sewing small items of appliqué. If you are stitching large areas of appliqué, or if you want to quilt a large piece of patchwork, a quilting frame is recommended.

An embroidery hoop consists of two rings, usually made from wood, which fit closely one within the other so that the fabric is kept evenly stretched. The outer ring has a screw attachment for adjusting the tension. A quilting hoop works in the same way, but is larger.

Slate embroidery and quilting frames come in different sizes and weights. They are usually made from wood and constructed in much the same way. They have two rollers with tapes attached and two stretchers with slots at the ends to take the rollers and a series of holes into which pegs or screws can be fitted. These are adjusted to give the right amount of tension to the fabric. The size of a frame is measured across the width of the tape. Both frames can be fitted with table or floor stands to leave both hands free for stitching.

Sewing Machines

A sewing machine is an excellent labour-saving piece of equipment useful for quick quilting, piecing patchwork blocks and stitching on appliqué patches, as well as for stitching very long seams needed in making up items and for many finishing processes.

For best results, choose a machine that will give a good straight stitch, and, if possible with a reverse stitch for starting and finishing, and a zigzag stitch for applying fabric patches and quick seaming.

Irons

An iron is an essential piece of equipment and a sound investment for any fabric craft. A thermostatically controlled steam iron generally gives the best results and is especially good for pressing seams really flat. It is quite important to have your iron and board close to your sewing area so that you can get used to the professional way of pressing seams as you sew. This makes the stitching much easier on complex pieces of patchwork.

Fabrics

Making a personal collection of fabrics is one of the most exciting aspects of working with fabric crafts, and plays an important part in the creative process of designing. Accidental arrangements of colours and patterns may trigger off new design ideas, often when least expected. All kinds of fibres in plain and mixed coloured patterns can be used. However, for patchwork and appliqué, certain fabrics work better than others.

Generally, smooth, closely woven fabrics such as dressweight cottons, brushed cottons, fine linen, lightweight wool, lawn, poplin, satin, silk or sateen work best. It is better to avoid synthetic, crease-resistant, or very stretchy fabrics as they are more difficult to handle. Heavier damasks, velvets,

BELOW A variety of needlework frames that can be used for quilting, appliqué and embroidery. The advantage of using a frame with a stand is that both hands are left free to work. The palette is used to keep lengths of thread tidy.

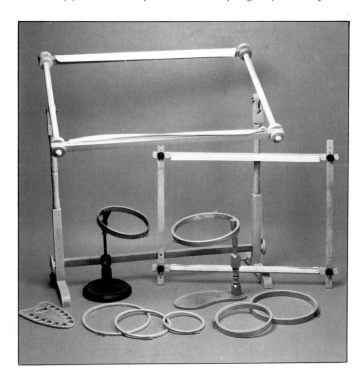

corduroys, suitings and tweeds combine well together and can be used for bigger machine-sewn projects.

Cotton fabrics should be pre-washed and ironed while still damp, to test for colour fastness and shrinkage. Avoid using any fabrics where the dyes may run.

Other more unusual fabrics suitable for certain types of patchwork or appliqué are felt, plastic-coated fabrics and leather, including suede, chamois and different hides. As turned-under hems are not required, items such as fashion garments, accessories, cushions, hangings and toys can be quickly machine-stitched. However, as leather and felt cannot be washed, the cleaning requirements should be considered before going ahead with a project.

BELOW Try to keep a selection of different fabrics for patchwork and appliqué; even tiny scraps may be useful. Then you will have a wide choice when you need fabrics which will tone with one another — or ones which will contrast.

16

Chapter Two
PATCHWORK

INTRODUCTION TO PATCHWORK

If you are not already familiar with what patchwork is, its alternative name, pieced work, gives you a clue! Patchwork consists of cutting out small pieces of different fabrics and stitching them together in a decorative pattern to produce a completely new 'fabric'. The decorative pattern may be produced by the shapes of the pieces, by the patterns of the original fabrics which can be carefully rearranged — for instance with stripes going in different directions — or by the arrangements of the different colours. The best pieces of patchwork take all three elements into account.

The First Patchwork

The origins of patchwork are lost in history. Examples of patchwork have been found in the Egyptian tombs and in archaeological remains on the old silk road between China and India, and it is conjectured that Joseph's coat of many colours in the Old Testament may have been patchwork. Certainly, patchwork items are known to have been brought back from the East by the Crusaders, but it was not until the 17th and 18th centuries, when the East India Trading Company started to import fine printed cotton into Britain, that patchwork became a fashionable pastime for leisured middle- and upper-class ladies.

The popularity of these imported Indian chintzes posed a threat to the British textile manufacturers who could not yet match the quality in colour and printing; they pressed for trade restrictions, making the fabrics scarce and expensive. Every tiny scrap was hoarded to be used in patchwork and appliqué, to make a little go a long way.

Alongside these fine quilts, made in scarce and expensive materials by the middle and the upper classes, was another type of patchwork made strictly for utilitarian purposes by the working classes. The materials used in these quilts were often homespun or the less expensive cotton fabrics manufactured and printed in Britain. Simple shapes such as triangles, squares and diamonds were pieced together with a running stitch.

Development of Designs

The settlement of North America was the next significant factor in the development of patchwork. Contrary to expectations, the first colonists found a hostile environment awaiting them. Basic supplies were short and to repair and recycle was the order of the day. Trade restrictions, which forced the colonists to buy fabrics from Britain, made them not just expensive but virtually unobtainable, so scraps of fabric were hoarded and used in the first American patchwork quilts. These were utilitarian and with little planned design. As life became more settled, the quilt makers began to develop the traditions and designs which were to become uniquely American.

Limited space in many homes meant that it made sense to construct a quilt in units which could be easily worked on the lap. Designs for these units, or 'blocks', were evolved first by folding paper. An additional advantage to this type of quilt construction was that the blocks could be stacked away ready for assembly when enough had been completed.

Patchwork Revival

In the early years of the 20th century patchwork suffered a decline; fabrics were more readily available and more reasonably priced, and there was no longer the need to hoard scraps of fabric. Then, with the revival of interest in many handicrafts that began in the late 60s and 70s, people began to realise the beauty of many of the traditional patchwork designs and also the craft's potential as a modern art form.

ABOVE Each block in this quilt uses the same English patchwork templates, but the different fabrics give the blocks quite different effects.

LEFT Patchwork isn't just a traditional craft, as this contemporary piece shows.

BELOW A square of American patchwork bound round the edges with matching fabrics.

Starting Patchwork

The intricate appearance of some patchwork designs may make it seem a complicated craft, but in fact the basic principles and techniques of patchwork are very simple indeed. As long as you are accurate with your fabric cutting and stitching, you will easily be able to produce good-quality patchwork pieces with your first attempts. Begin with some of the easier patterns, and as your confidence grows you will quickly be able to try larger pieces and more complex patterns.

Types of Patchwork

Patchwork is traditionally divided into two types; pieced and applied. Pieced patchwork involves stitching individual pieces of fabric together in different arrangements, and may be done by the English method (using paper templates) or the American method (where geometric shapes are stitched together with ordinary seams). Applied patchwork involves stitching small pieces of fabric onto a larger piece of backing fabric; there are many different methods of applied patchwork.

DESIGNING YOUR PATCHWORK

Before you begin cutting out pieces of fabric, it's best to spend a little time planning out your patchwork design. You will want to think of the purpose you are going to put it to; for instance, a piece of patchwork for a cot quilt will want to be in different colours, fabrics and patterns from a piece of crazy patchwork for a playroom curtain.

If your patchwork design is based on squares and triangles you can plan the shapes and colour combinations out on squared graph paper. Try out different design layouts for hexagons, stars, diamonds and triangles on isometric graph paper. These shapes can be used singly or in combination. Isometric paper is marked out in a grid of triangles, and can also be used for making the papers which are tacked into the fabric patches, and for tracing accurate templates. Sort scrap fabrics into colour groups or tone values so that you can impose some order on your designs, or use a common fabric as a background or border.

Estimating Fabric Quantity

This is not always easy, especially if oddments are included, but an approximate calculation can be made once you have cut the templates to size and counted how many different patches are needed.

Using a fabric width of 90cm (36in) and a 10cm (4in) square template, for example, calculate how many

TOP RIGHT Designs involving squares, rectangles and triangles can be drawn up first on ordinary squared graph paper so that you can plot out how you want the colours and patterns to relate. This will also help you to estimate how many shapes you will need from each fabric, and how many paper templates if you are using the template method.

LEFT Isometric graph paper is based on equilateral triangles, and is very good for plotting patchwork designs based on triangles, hexagons and diamonds. Because all of these shapes interlock, you can use the graph paper to experiment with different combinations.

RIGHT This patchwork quilt was made in England at the beginning of the century, using some of the patterned chintzes that were very popular at the time. Each octagon has been cut so that it frames a large flower, which has added to the overall attractiveness of the design. If your patchwork fabrics feature strong motifs, you can give your design extra effect by framing the motifs in the patchwork shapes in the same way.

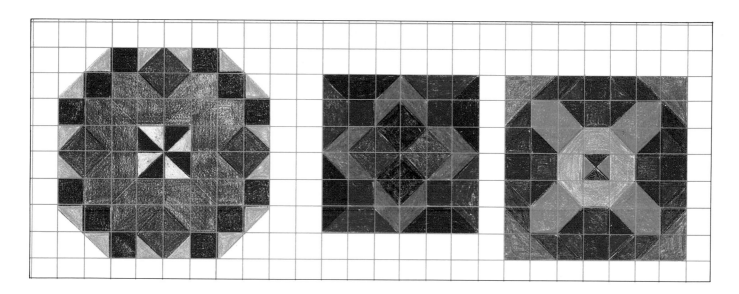

shapes can be cut from one width (90 ÷ 10 = 9). If you require 80 blocks, for example, calculate the length needed by dividing this number by the number of times the template fits across the fabric and multiply the figure by the depth of the template (80 ÷ 9 = 9 [rounded up] × 10cm = 90cm). You will need 90cm (36in) of 90cm (36in) wide fabric. Bear in mind that certain templates, such as the hexagon and the triangle, can be more economically placed than others. Calculate border strips in the same way.

Marking and Cutting Fabric

Position the templates and lightly mark all cutting lines on the wrong side of the fabric, using an appropriately coloured pencil. Make sure you place the templates on the straight grain of the fabric, avoiding the bias grain. Reverse asymmetric shapes, such as the trapezoid, so that they appear the correct way round when stitched together. Cut out the patches separately using very sharp scissors.

Sewing Pieced Blocks Together

Before sewing, lay out your patches to check the overall design. Certain hand-sewn patterns may vary slightly, but in general it is good practice first to join small units, such as triangles, to form squares (and then join the squares progressively into bigger blocks, and so on). Finally, assemble the larger units to form rows across and then stitch the rows together. Add strips between or borders as needed. Once you have established the sequence for making a block, continue with it for all the blocks in the same pattern.

Machine Sewing

While most patterns involving simple triangles, squares and rectangles can be pieced quite successfully by machine, curves and some complicated geometric shapes are better stitched by hand.

USING TEMPLATES

The sewing method will determine the type of patchwork template you need. For the English method of patchwork, where the pieces of fabric are tacked over papers and overstitched together, the basic template for cutting out the paper pieces should be the size of the finished patch.

Templates for hand-sewn patchwork, such as the clamshell, hexagon and diamond, can be bought from craft shops in a range of sizes. They are made from thin metal or plastic and are produced either as two solid shapes, one 6mm ($\frac{1}{4}$in) larger than the other all round, or as a window template where the outer edge is 6mm ($\frac{1}{4}$in) from the inner edge. In each case, the larger shape is used to cut out the fabric and the smaller shape, or the inner edge, is used for cutting out the backing papers. This gives a 6mm ($\frac{1}{4}$in) seam allowance all round the fabric patch.

If you cannot buy the one you need it is possible to make one with a basic geometry set. Any shape or combination of shapes which fit together without leaving a gap (tessellate) can be used in English patchwork. The need for accuracy cannot be stressed enough when making templates. Use a sharp hard pencil (2H) to draw with and cut the template from stiff (though not thick) card using a craft knife and metal ruler.

RIGHT A selection of the geometric patchwork templates available commercially. You will see that not all of the shapes will interlink (tessellate) with all of the other shapes.

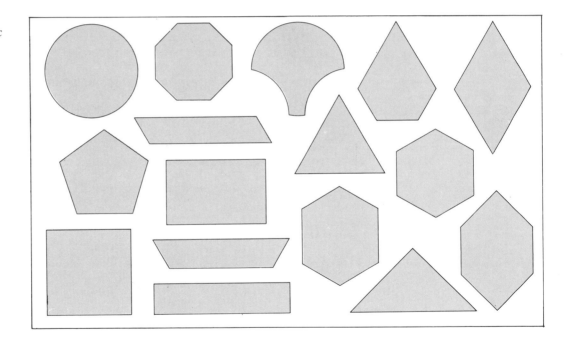

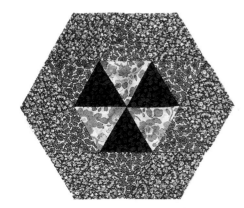

ABOVE These samples show how templates of different shapes can be combined to make further shapes. The designs were planned on isometric graph paper so that the interlinking of the shapes could be checked.

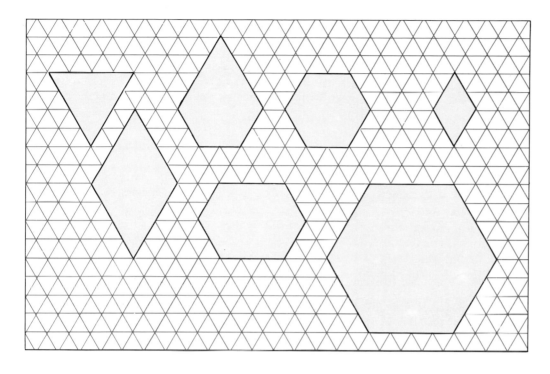

LEFT *These diagrams show how isometric graph paper can be used as a cutting guide for certain template shapes. You can cut your paper templates as well as master templates from the isometric paper.*

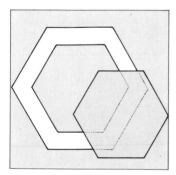

ABOVE Window templates allow you to position a motif in the centre of your patchwork patch. The inside section of the template is clear, allowing you to see through to the fabric pattern underneath; you move the template around until the motif is in the required position, and then cut the fabric around the guidelines provided by the template edges.

BACKING AND JOINING PATCHES

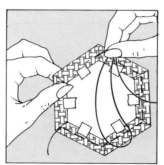

1 *Place paper template on fabric, wrong side up. Secure with a pin, and fold each edge tightly over. Anchor edges with adhesive tape.*

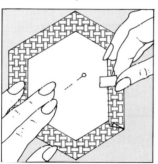

2 *Tack round the edges of the fabric to hold it down over the paper, taking care not to penetrate the paper itself. Keep the fabric pulled taut throughout.*

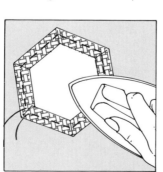

3 *Remove the adhesive tape, and press each patch on the wrong side to ensure sharp clean folds. This stage is vital in achieving a well-finished item.*

4 *Lay two patches together, right sides inwards, and overstitch them neatly together along one edge. Do not remove tacking until hexagon is completely surrounded.*

CRAZY PATCHWORK

HAND-SEWN

Crazy patchwork (or puzzle patchwork) was a favourite pastime devised by the Victorians as a means of using small scraps of the rich and beautiful fabrics then in fashion — from silks, satins, velvets and brocades to many brightly coloured and inexpensive printed cottons and chintzes.

The patchwork was made with an all-over design where patches were overlapped and stitched to a foundation fabric almost regardless of size and colour. Typical colours included many dark reds and blues, bright golden yellows and black. The raw edges were then lavishly embroidered with herringbone or feather stitches in a twisted thread, usually in the same rich, golden yellow. Quite frequently, the patches were also embroidered with strong, vibrant colours, beads, metallic threads and sequins. Throws, pelmets, cushions and cosies were made, and the edges scalloped, satin frilled, fringed or corded to give a colourful and energetic form of Victorian over-decoration. The work was always lined and tied randomly.

Old and New

This is the perfect technique for indulging sentiment. If, for example, you have a collection of old fabrics, oddments of real lace, embroidered motifs, ribbons, mottoes, woven labels, even pretty buttons and braids, they can all be worked into a keepsake patchwork, in true Victorian style. Alternatively, much contemporary patchwork is made with the sewing machine, using zigzag stitch to cover the edges or straight stitch for turned-in edges.

RIGHT This American quilt is a typical example of crazy patchwork. A rich variety of fabrics has been used, further embellished by the use of surface stitches to embroider small motifs, and the ornamentation of the seams of the pieced fabric by a variety of stitches, including variations of feather, herringbone, and buttonhole. The quilt is made up of a series of square blocks of crazy patchwork and bits of Dresden Plate design, joined together and surrounded by a striking decorative border.

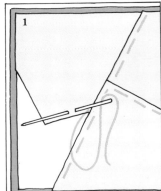

1 Beginning in one corner, arrange the unfinished patches on the foundation fabric, overlapping the edges, and secure with small running stitches.

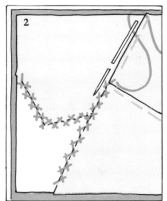

2 Complete all the patches in this way, and then cover the edges with either herringbone, double or triple feather, blanket stitch or couching.

ABQVE The Victorian love of elaborate decoration can be seen in this example of crazy patchwork, made with different coloured scraps of silk and satin. The surface is covered with couched metallic cord, sequins and beads.

CRAZY PATCHWORK

MACHINE-SEWN

Crazy Patchwork is very easy to do by sewing machine, too. As the patches don't have to be even sizes and shapes they can simply be stitched to the background fabric with wide zigzag or satin stitch, and of course you can easily stitch round curves and jagged edges which is virtually impossible with template patchwork. Stitching by machine is very quick, and a machine-stitched crazy patchwork quilt could be produced in a day with no difficulty.

Stained Glass

A colourful variation on crazy patchwork is to produce a stained glass window effect by covering the joins between the patches of fabric with black tape and machining it into place. If you use bias binding, the binding can be curved around difficult shapes; or you can cut your patches so that the sides are all straight lines, even if the patches are not regular sizes and shapes. Another way to produce this effect is with bands of wide satin stitch along the seam lines; this stitching could be in any colour.

Fancy Stitches

If your sewing machine does fancy stitches, you could use these along the seam lines instead of zigzag. This effect imitates the decorative stitching that the Victorians worked by hand along the joins of their crazy patchwork patterns.

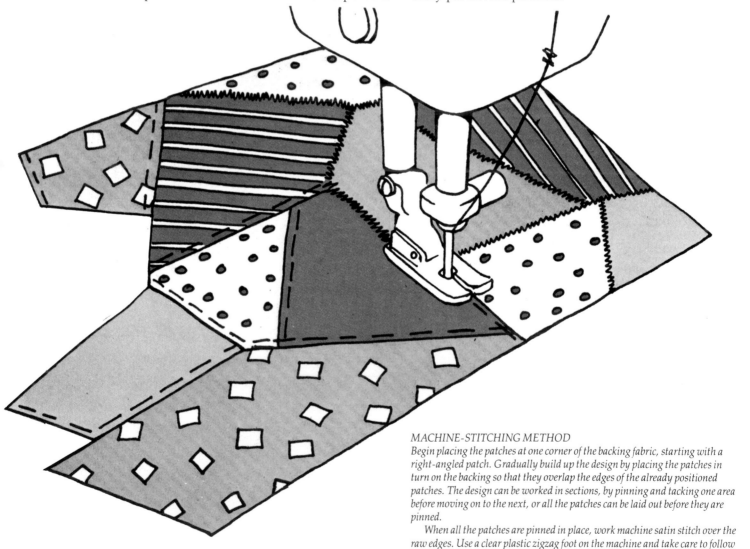

MACHINE-STITCHING METHOD
Begin placing the patches at one corner of the backing fabric, starting with a right-angled patch. Gradually build up the design by placing the patches in turn on the backing so that they overlap the edges of the already positioned patches. The design can be worked in sections, by pinning and tacking one area before moving on to the next, or all the patches can be laid out before they are pinned.

When all the patches are pinned in place, work machine satin stitch over the raw edges. Use a clear plastic zigzag foot on the machine and take care to follow the outlines accurately.

ABOVE This contemporary patchwork shows the stained glass technique of edging each patch with a border of wide satin stitch.

SQUARES AND RECTANGLES

Squares and rectangles are the easiest possible patchwork shapes to start with. One enormous advantage is that they can easily be joined by hand or machine! Even with these simple shapes, there are many ways in which colours and patterns can be combined to produce a pleasing design.

Patches can either be made with backing papers, or can be joined with machine seams as long as the patches are not too small and you stitch the seams accurately. A 6cm (2½in) square is a popular size for wall hangings, cot or crib quilts, cushions, and other soft furnishing uses, but it can be adjusted to suit other items as required. Fabric games-boards are fun to make using alternate light and dark square patches.

Plain fabrics or those with very small prints, or fine shirting fabrics such as dressweight cottons, lawn, brushed cotton, wool mixes or medium-weight silks, work well with square and rectangular patches. Before you begin cutting out, make a scaled drawing of your finished design on graph paper and indicate the fabrics you will be using. Keep the chart at hand so that you can refer to it when you are cutting the shapes and piecing the design.

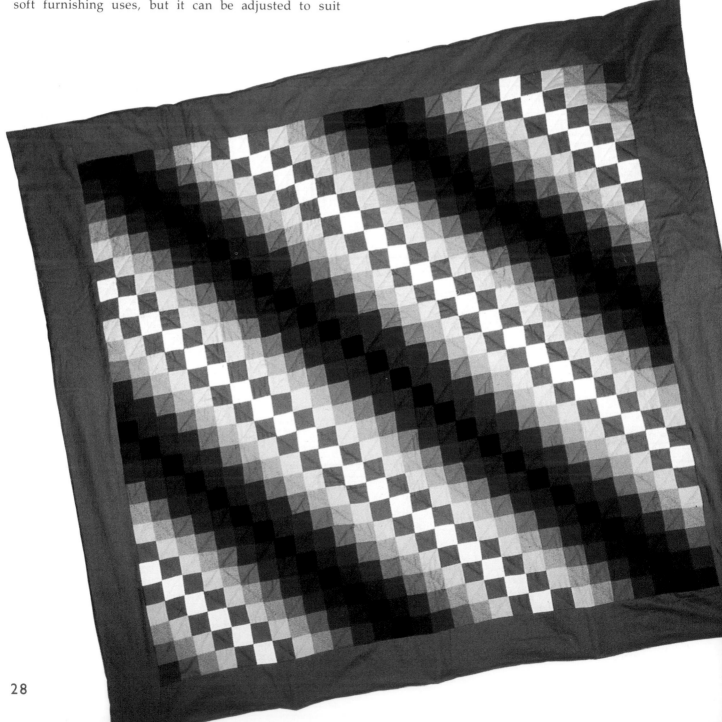

DESIGNS WITH SQUARES AND RECTANGLES
1 Rectangular Hit and Miss
2 Square Hit and Miss
3 Castellations
4 Framed Squares

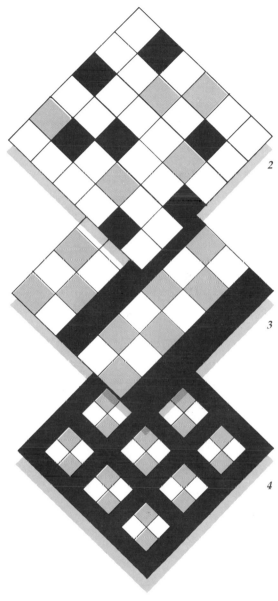

JOINING SQUARE AND
RECTANGULAR PATCHES
1 *The patches can be joined by the*
ordinary template method; tack the
fabric over the paper templates, then
stitch together by hand.
2 *and* **3** *If you want to join squares or*
rectangles by machine, stitch them
together in rows with even-sized
seams. Then join the rows together
with long seams.

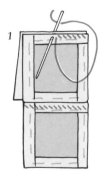

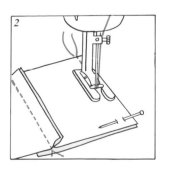

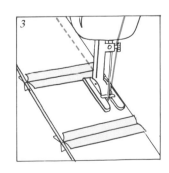

LEFT *This piece of patchwork was made from squares in a simple stepped*
diagonal pattern, but its range of shaded toning colours is very effective.

HEXAGONS

GRANDMOTHER'S GARDEN

Hexagons are some of the most popular shapes for English patchwork, and one of the easiest patterns to do with them is the one known as Grandmother's Garden, or Grandmother's Flower Garden. In this design, the hexagons are stitched together in rosettes of seven patches, often with a contrasting fabric used for the central patch so that the rosettes resemble flowers. The rosettes are then stitched to each other or applied to a backing fabric in different combinations.

DRAWING A HEXAGON TEMPLATE

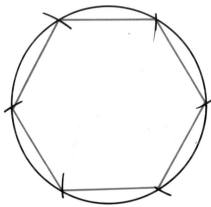

Set the compasses to the desired length of the hexagon's sides and draw a circle. Using the same radius, place the compass point anywhere on the circle and draw an arc crossing the circle's circumference. Now place the compass point on the crossing point and draw another arc. Continue around the circle until you have 6 crosses. Join these with straight lines to form a hexagon. Make one card or acetate template and use it as a master shape for all your paper templates; make a larger one with seam allowances added, and use it as a cutting guide for your fabric patches.

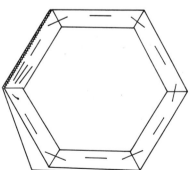

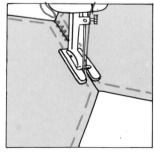

MAKING THE ROSETTES

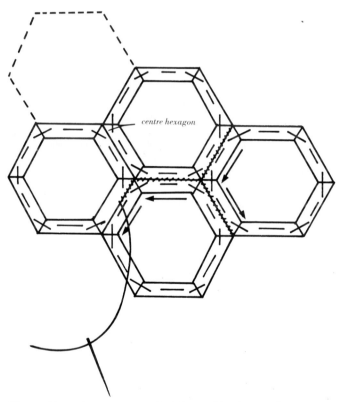

centre hexagon

When making up hexagon rosettes, begin by attaching the centre hexagon to one of the side hexagons. Take a third hexagon and continue stitching with the same thread round the corner to join the second and third hexagons. With a new piece of thread attach the second side of the centre hexagon to the third patch and continue round the corner to attach the fourth hexagon. Continue in this way until the rosette is complete. Make sure that your stitching goes right into each corner so that there are no gaps.

JOINING THE PATCHES
1 To join patches by hand, begin with a knot or with 2-3 stitches on top of each other. Hold two patches with their right sides together and oversew neatly; finish off with several firm backstitches.

2 To join hexagons by machine, hold the patches together side by side, right sides up, and stitch along the join with zigzag stitching.

26 + 20

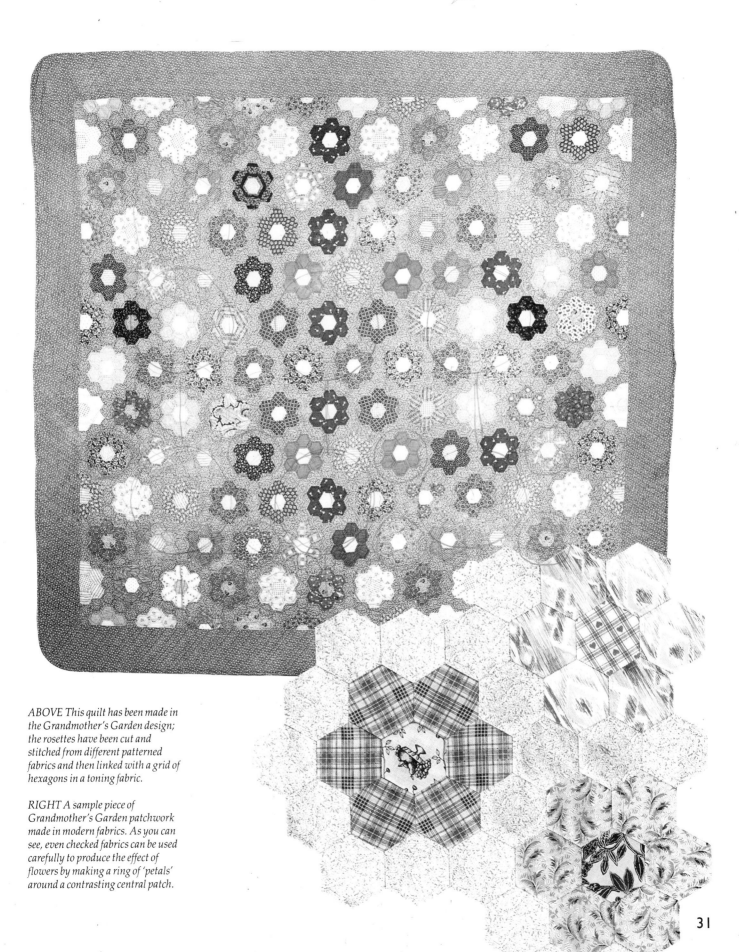

ABOVE This quilt has been made in the Grandmother's Garden design; the rosettes have been cut and stitched from different patterned fabrics and then linked with a grid of hexagons in a toning fabric.

RIGHT A sample piece of Grandmother's Garden patchwork made in modern fabrics. As you can see, even checked fabrics can be used carefully to produce the effect of flowers by making a ring of 'petals' around a contrasting central patch.

31

HEXAGONS

FINISHING AND BACKING

Because hexagon patchwork leaves an irregularly-shaped edge, there are various different ways in which you can finish off the edges of your project. You might want to exploit the irregular edges and make a shaped backing to match them, or you might decide to use one of the various ways of butting the hexagons up to a straight edge.

RIGHT When you have stitched all the hexagons together, turn the patchwork over and remove all of the backing papers apart from those in the hexagons round the very edges. The edge papers can then be removed one by one as you finish the borders of the patchwork.

BELOW
STRAIGHT BORDER METHODS
There are several alternative ways of producing a straight border with hexagon patchwork.
1 Use segments of the hexagons to fill out the irregular edges.
2 Appliqué the finished patchwork onto a straight border, by hand or machine.
3 Cut the edges of the patchwork to produce a straight edge, turn under the edges, and either stitch onto backing fabric with conventional seam or appliqué.

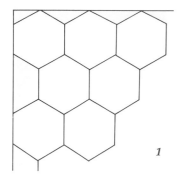

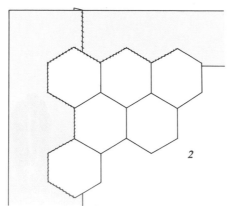

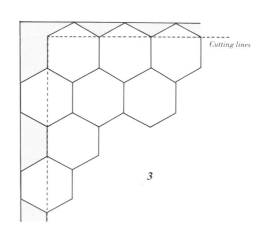

Cutting lines

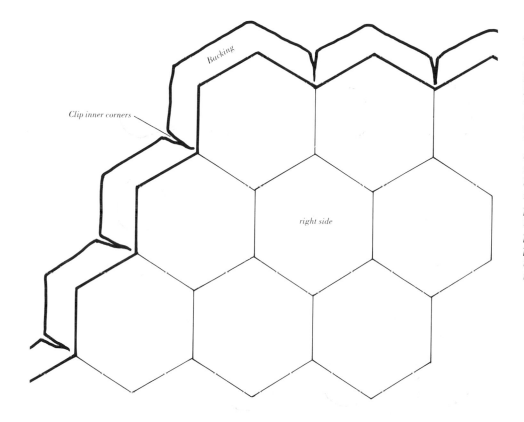

Backing

Clip inner corners

right side

MAKING A SHAPED BACKING
To shape the backing to the outer hexagons press the outer edges of the patchwork and carefully remove the papers. Cut the backing fabric, 3.5cm (1½in) larger than the quilt top all round, and tack the top and backing together with wrong sides facing. Trim the backing fabric round the shaped edge 9mm (⅜in) larger all round. Clip the inner corners on the backing fabric so that when turned in it will lie flat against the back of the patchwork. Turn in the backing so that the folded edges of the patchwork and backing match up, pin, tack and slip hem the edges together. Quilt if desired, and remove tacking.

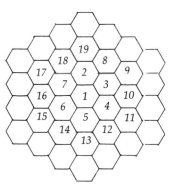

DOUBLE ROSETTES
You can also make a Grandmother's Garden design with double rosettes, as shown here. Join patches 2-7 round the central rosette first, then add patches 8-19 as a second border.

DIAMONDS

The acute angles at the points of diamonds make them a little more difficult to handle than hexagons, but if you tuck the fabric in carefully when you are tacking them you will find that they join accurately. Diamonds can be used to produce stars, hexagons and the 3-D effect pattern known as Tumbling Blocks; you will also find that you can make patchwork pieces with diamonds that are fatter or narrower, although if you alter the angles the diamonds you produce won't interlink with regular hexagons.

RIGHT A section of Tumbling Blocks patchwork, showing the characteristic arrangement of light, medium and dark fabrics.

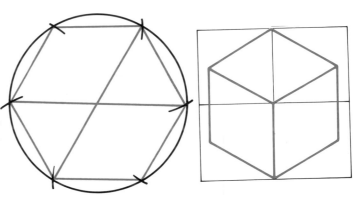

DRAWING DIAMOND TEMPLATES
Two methods of producing accurate diamond templates from hexagons are shown here.

1 Connect opposite points to form two diamonds and two equilateral triangles.
2 Draw radii in from three corners of the hexagon to the centre, to produce three diamonds.

TACKING IN THE PAPERS

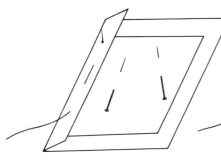 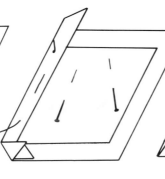 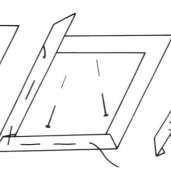 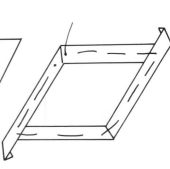

1 The grain of the fabric is dictated by how the pieces are to be set in the quilt. Start tacking at one of the wide angles.

2 Fold down the excess fabric at the acute angle.

3 Continue tacking and folding down the corners; finish off with one or two backstitches.

4 If fabric is bulky fold once only when tacking to paper.

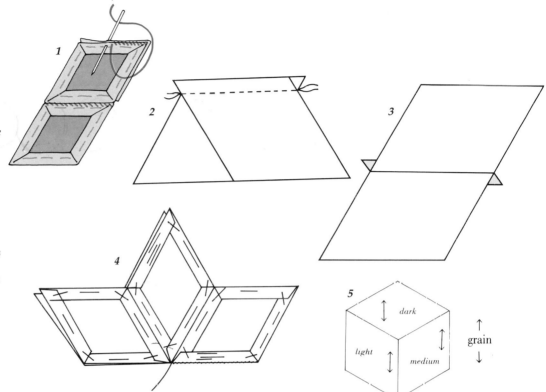

JOINING DIAMONDS

1 To join diamonds by hand, work with paper templates in the patches. Place two patches right sides together and oversew the seam with tiny stitches.

2 and **3** To join diamonds by machine you do not need paper templates provided that you mark and stitch the seams carefully. Place two patches right sides together so that the points overlap as shown, then stitch an ordinary seam.

4 When making a six-pointed star, sew the diamonds together in two sets of three, then sew the two halves of the star together across the centre seam. This avoids the possibility of a gap forming where the diamonds all join in the centre.

5 For the Tumbling Blocks pattern, join the diamonds into hexagons, keeping the arrangements of the tones consistent in each hexagon. Then join the hexagon shapes together.

LEFT This spectacular star quilt shows how effective diamonds can be; the shapes have been arranged in radiating rings of colour, and smaller stars have been pieced to decorate the corners of the quilt.

TRIANGLES

Triangles are some of the simplest shapes to join, and like diamonds they have the advantage that they can be joined by hand or by machine. You can build up a pattern by using identical triangles throughout, by using triangles of different sizes and angles, or by combining triangles with other template shapes. Make sure that you keep all the points really crisp so that the patchwork lies flat when all the patches are joined.

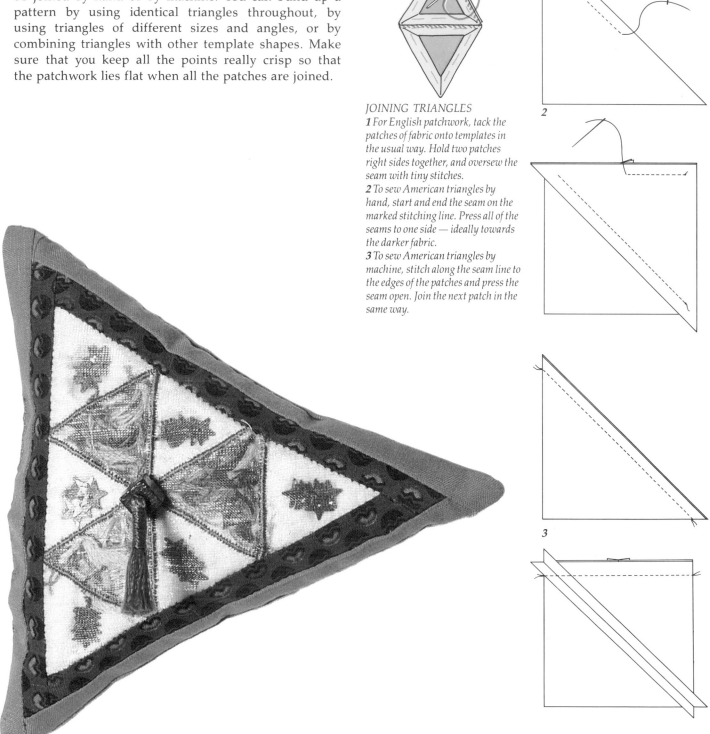

JOINING TRIANGLES

1 For English patchwork, tack the patches of fabric onto templates in the usual way. Hold two patches right sides together, and oversew the seam with tiny stitches.

2 To sew American triangles by hand, start and end the seam on the marked stitching line. Press all of the seams to one side — ideally towards the darker fabric.

3 To sew American triangles by machine, stitch along the seam line to the edges of the patches and press the seam open. Join the next patch in the same way.

LEFT Triangles don't have to be built into squares; this pincushion has made the most of the triangle shape.

ABOVE An extensive collection of scrap fabrics has been put to good use in this triangle quilt. The triangles have been stitched together so that they form alternate diamonds of light and dark fabrics.

CLAMSHELL

Clamshell patchwork gets its name from the overlapping shell shapes used to produce the patterns, and is one of the oldest patchwork designs known.

The technique involves hand sewing rows of overlapping shells in patterns or in a random way, either with or without a foundation fabric. Each shell is carefully cut out using a template and made with a backing paper to ensure a perfectly curved outline. As the patches are stitched from the right side, it is crucial that the edges are accurately curved since there is no other seaming to help disguise any imperfections. If you have a sewing machine with a swing needle, you may prefer to experiment by zigzag stitching the patches together.

Smooth-textured, fine cottons in patterned or plain colours are best for making the patches. You will need contrasting colours for designs such as chevrons, diagonal stripes and diamonds; mixed plain and patterned prints for random placing; graduated toning fabrics for shaded effects.

Clamshell patchwork works particularly well on small items like tea- and coffee-pot cosies, bags, bolsters and cushions, as well as on larger quilts and coverlets. Larger items should be lined and tied to keep the layers together.

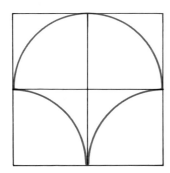

MAKING A CLAMSHELL TEMPLATE
Draw a square with sides the same length as you want the height of your clamshell. Divide it into quarters, and use compasses to draw a semicircle through the top half and to produce two quarter-circles in the bottom squares.

JOINING CLAMSHELL PATCHES

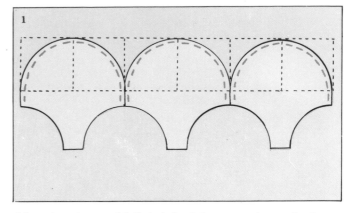

1 Lay out your top row of shells, tacked to their paper templates, and make sure that they are exactly level. Slip-stitch them to the backing fabric around the curves, and remove the paper templates.

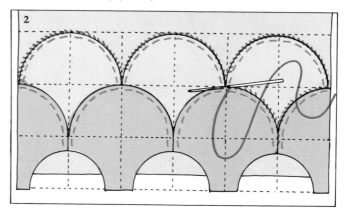

2 Place the next row in position over the first row, and attach in the same way.

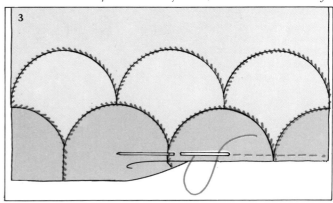

3 When you have finished the rows, remove the final templates and tack the raw edges under ready for finishing.

SUFFOLK PUFFS

Suffolk Puffs are gathered circular patches which are handsewn together with the edges touching and leaving small spaces in between. The most effective fabrics to use are fine ones such as silk, soft cotton voile or organdie. The gathered side of the circle is the right side and the central hole creates a decorative, textural effect. This simple technique can be varied in several ways: combine puffs of different sizes in one project or place a decorative filling in transparent puffs. The gathering thread need not be pulled tight, thus showing the inside of the patch, which could be padded or filled with a contrasting colour, or stitched varying the length of the connecting stitches.

BELOW Suffolk Puffs have been made in translucent fabric and the silk gathering threads have been left dangling in this delicate piece of modern patchwork.

MAKING THE PUFFS

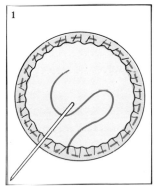

1 Begin by cutting circles of fabric about twice the diameter of the finished patch. Fold over 6mm (¼in) to the wrong side, and use a strong thread, firmly secured, to work a ring of even gathering stitches around the rim.

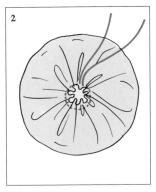

2 Pull the gathering thread up tightly, flatten the puff so that the gathered edge is in the middle, and fasten off the thread. The puffs can be used with the gathered section at the front of the work, or with it hidden underneath.

SUGAR BOWL

The Sugar Bowl design is a favourite old American pattern, and one of many variations each with its own evocative name such as Drunkard's Path, Fool's Puzzle, Falling Timbers and Wonder of the World. This is a four-patch pattern where each patch is made up of two units: a small square with a quarter circle set in one corner — the curved seam being best hand sewn. The patches are pieced together so that the four corners form a circle within a larger square block.

Traditionally, two colours are used but mixed colours arranged as in this contemporary quilt can be very attractive — an excellent scrap-bag design. Here pretty prints salvaged from discarded dresses have been cleverly designed and pieced into a large symmetrical pattern with a random effect. Similar designs could be planned with mixed colours but using fewer prints; spots with sprig prints and plain colours; stripes with spots and plains; plaids with tiny checks and plain colours would all give interesting results. This kind of imposed restriction often helps in planning a design.

Dressweight cotton, cotton/wool mixes and fine silks are ideal for Sugar Bowl patchwork. Its reasonably large repeat is suitable for soft furnishings — curtains, cushions, floor seating, sofa throws and table covers.

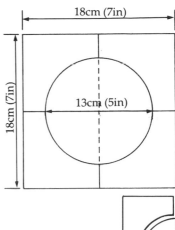

18cm (7in)

18cm (7in)

13cm (5in)

MAKING
SUGAR BOWL PATCHES

*To make the patch, clip the convex
curve on the quarter circle, and
assemble the two units right sides
inside and curves together, with the
quarter circle unit below. Pin the
corners first and then ease the fabric
as you pin around the curve. Sew the
curve by hand and the straight seams
by machine, if preferred.*

*Make up the four patches of each
block and join them together. Lay
them out in pattern and join the
blocks into rows across and then into
a complete patchwork.*

*ABOVE Each square patch in this Sugar Bowl design has been made with two
fabrics; each fabric in the patch is used for two outer shapes and two
quarter-circles.*

DRESDEN PLATE

TEMPLATES

Dresden Plate is a very pretty patchwork design which lends itself equally well to traditional or modern interpretations. Each 'plate' is built up from several petal shapes and then appliquéd to the background fabric. Dresden Plate designs are ideal for small projects like cushion covers and shoulder bags, when just one 'plate' can be used, or the design can be used for quite large projects with the 'plates' arranged in an attractive composition on a plain background.

Firm, evenly woven fabrics are best for Dresden Plate designs; it is particularly important with this design to make sure that the fabrics are washed before they are used, as the 'plates' will pull badly out of shape if the fabrics shrink when the piece of patchwork is washed. You can use a different fabric for every petal shape, or repeat the same fabrics in each quarter of the circle, or you can work round in a rainbow very effectively. For a very contemporary look, you could alternate strong colours around the circle.

DRESDEN PLATE TEMPLATES

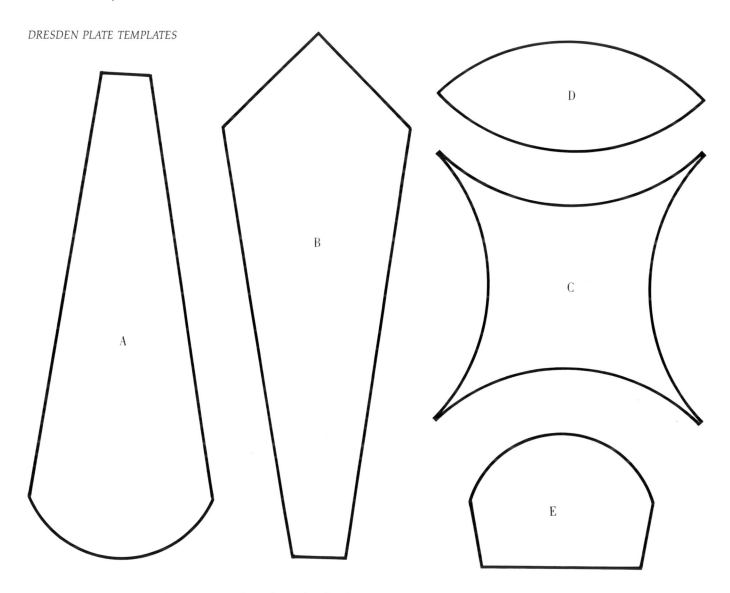

The templates for Dresden Plate designs vary according to the number of petal shapes around the circle. Each petal is a segment of a circle, so the wider the segment the fewer petals you need to complete the pattern. Both of these templates produce a plate with 20 segments, but you could draw your own wider or narrower ones for more or fewer petals in the circle. Template A is the traditional shape for Dresden Plate templates, with a curved tip; template B is a variation on the basic design which gives pointed tips to each petal shape.

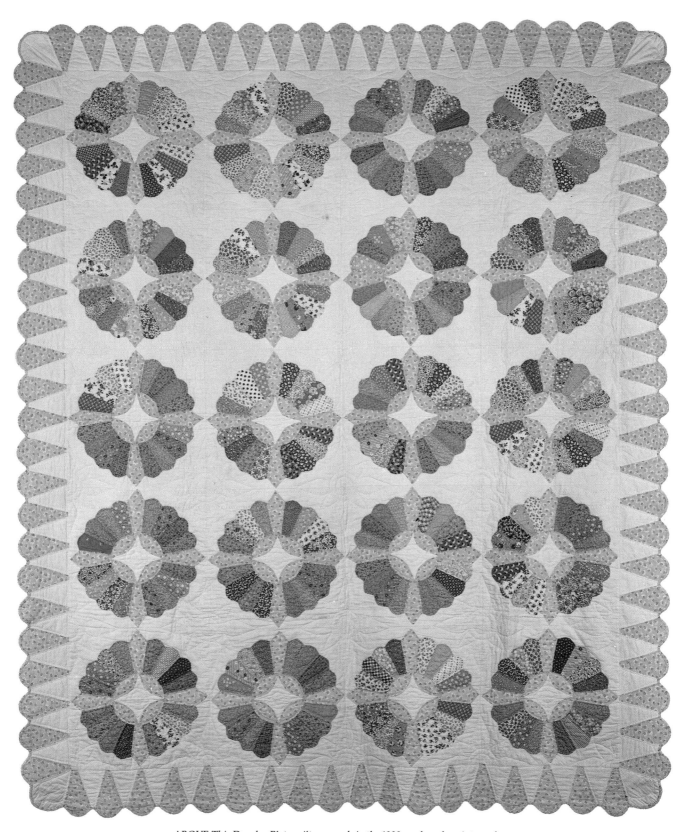

ABOVE This Dresden Plate quilt was made in the 1930s and used a mixture of rounded and pointed templates to imitate some of the sunray motifs that were particularly popular during the Art Deco era. You could use the templates on the opposite page to reproduce this quilt or a similar one; cut 16 rounded petals and 4 pointed ones, and use 4 patches cut from template D round a middle patch cut from template C. Template E will give you a curved shape which can be used for backing the curved petals around the border.

DRESDEN PLATE

METHOD

PREPARING PATCHES FOR DRESDEN PLATE

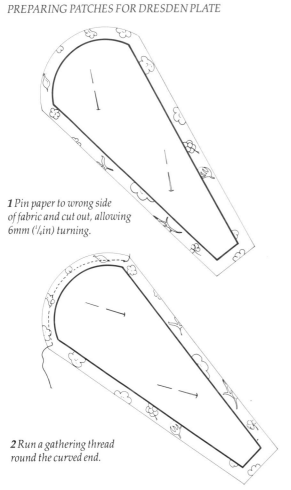

1 *Pin paper to wrong side of fabric and cut out, allowing 6mm (¹/₄in) turning.*

2 *Run a gathering thread round the curved end.*

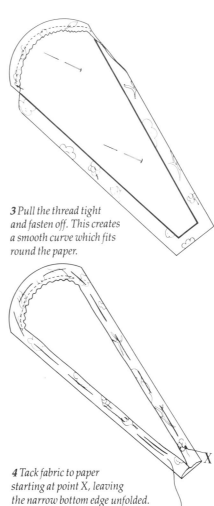

3 *Pull the thread tight and fasten off. This creates a smooth curve which fits round the paper.*

4 *Tack fabric to paper starting at point X, leaving the narrow bottom edge unfolded.*

RIGHT Sampler quilts are excellent projects for groups, and good ways for beginners to try out different patchwork patterns. You can choose a different design for each block, then mount them all with frames or strips of fabric. This sampler quilt has several blocks which are worked in Dresden Plate variations.

BLOCKS

METHOD

American Patchwork is stitched without integral templates, and is usually made up into blocks. The blocks may be used on their own, or built up into large quilts featuring many blocks. Over the years many beautiful block patterns have emerged, some abstract or simple geometric designs, some stylised versions of an object such as a basket of flowers. Block designs are generally subdivided into smaller units or patches, which are pieced first and then stitched together to make the complete block; designs are often '4-patch' or '9-patch', which means that they are assembled into 4 or 9 smaller patches before being stitched into the complete block.

Cutting the Fabrics

When making up blocks in American patchwork the grain of the fabric should run parallel with the straight sides of the block. Mark a straight line on each template to indicate how you will position it on the fabric. Place the template on the wrong side of your fabric, remembering to turn over any asymmetrical template, for example, a rhomboid, so as not to cut a mirror image patch. Draw around each template with a fabric marker leaving enough space between them to add seam allowances when cutting out. Since the line you have marked is the stitching line, cut out each shape adding 6mm (¼in) all around the marked line. You can either draw the cutting line onto the fabric or measure by eye. When you have cut out all the patches in one block, place them together on a flat surface in the correct positions.

ABOVE An Amish quilt made in Iowa in the 1920s. Amish block designs are generally very simple, strong geometrical patterns.

Stitching by Hand

When hand-stitching patches together, use a neat running stitch on the marked sewing lines of each piece. Place the patches to be joined right sides together and match the lines with pins. The stitching should start and end at each seam line (not the edge of the fabric, see diagram) and should always start with a small knot or backstitch and finish firmly with a backstitch or two to prevent the seams from coming undone. Waxing will prevent the thread from knotting to some extent. Seam allowances should be pressed to one side, to the darker side of the seam where possible. When quilted this makes stronger seams and prevents the stitches from bulging open.

Stitching by Machine

Patches cut with templates made for machine piecing already have the seam allowance added. Piecing order follows the same principles as for hand stitched patchwork — smaller patches into larger ones and straight lines of stitching where possible. Machine-stitched seams are stronger and can be pressed open. Place patches right sides together and guide the raw edge against the presser foot — most sewing machines will give a 6mm (¼in) seam allowance. If yours does not, mark the plate on your machine parallel to the seam line and 6mm (¼in) from the needle using a narrow strip of masking tape and use that as a seam guide.

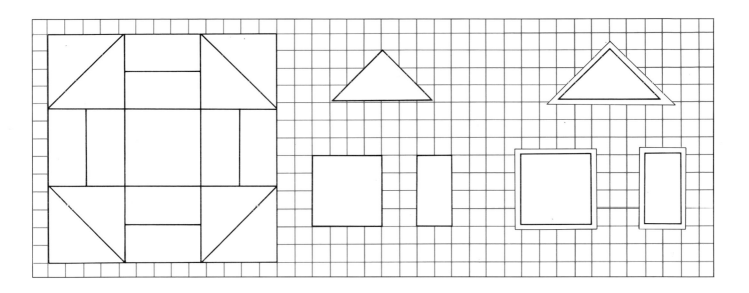

MAKING TEMPLATES FOR BLOCK DESIGNS

1 Draw a square the size you want your finished block to be and divide it into the correct grid (for instance, this is a '9-patch' grid). Now draw in the block pattern and identify how many different shaped templates you will need. In this example three different templates are needed: a square, a rectangle and a triangle.
2 Cut out each of the shapes needed from your full-size drawing and stick them onto card; these are now sturdy templates which can be used for cutting your fabrics.
3 As you cut your fabrics you will need to add 6mm ($^1/_4$in) seam allowance round the edges of each template as you cut. You can either draw this in on the fabrics in soft pencil, or cut the extra by eye.

STITCHING INTO A CORNER

If you are sewing a block in which it is necessary to stitch into a corner to set in a piece, pin the first two edges to be stitched together (the two that create the corner) and sew up to the seam allowance (not to the edge of the fabric), then sew the third piece to one side of the angle up to the corner, pivot the fabric and continue sewing the second part of the seam.

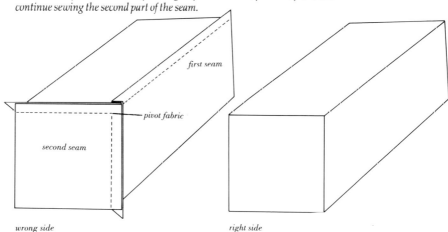

first seam

pivot fabric

second seam

wrong side

right side

PIECING ANGLED SHAPES

When joining shapes that run at an angle, other than a right angle, eg. diamonds and triangles, align the stitching lines, not the cut edges. This makes a straight edge when the patches are opened.

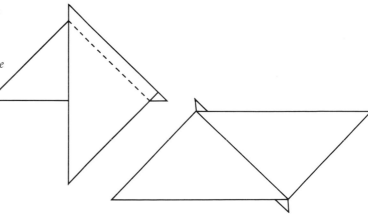

BLOCKS

ASSEMBLING THE BLOCKS

The two basic rules of piecing blocks are that you begin with the smallest pieces, and you stitch in straight lines whenever possible. Most designs can be subdivided into a number of smaller blocks or patches, so these are stitched first then assembled into the complete block.

STITCHING TRIANGLES INTO A RECTANGLE
The steps illustrated here show the sequence for joining one large and two small triangles to make an accurate rectangle.

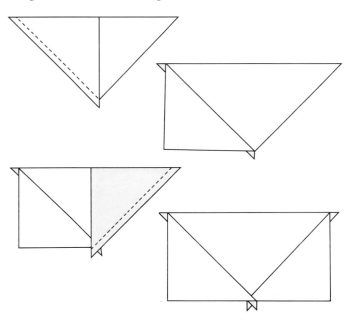

MATCHING POINTS
Some blocks have a point at which four or more fabrics meet. To match these points accurately, push a pin through at the exact spot where the points are to be matched at a right angle to your stitching. Stitch up to the pin, remove carefully and stitch over the point.

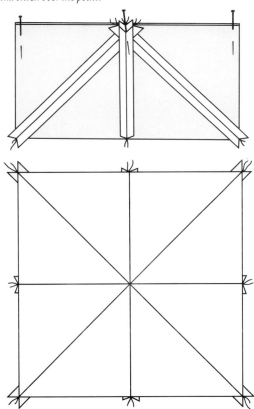

PIECING ORDER FOR 4-PATCH DESIGN
This design is one of many 4-patch block patterns. A similar sequence is followed for other 4-patch designs, even though the shapes of the individual elements will be different.

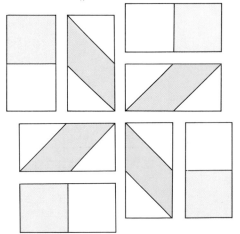

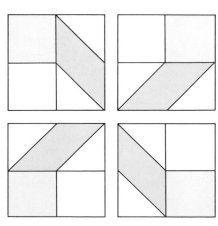

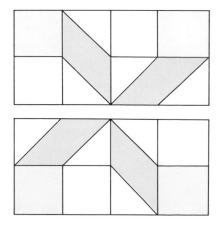

1 The smallest pieces are joined in straight seams; in this example they form 8 rectangles.

2 These patches are joined together with straight seams to form the basic 4 patches of the design.

3 The patches are joined in pairs, then the final central seam is stitched.

PIECING ORDER FOR 9-PATCH DESIGN
This design is a basic 9-patch pattern. A similar sequence is followed for other 9-patch designs, even though the shapes of the individual elements will be different.

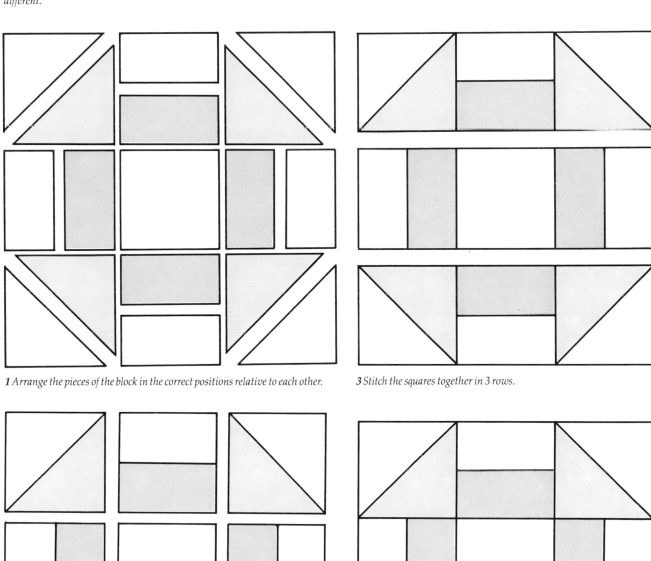

1 Arrange the pieces of the block in the correct positions relative to each other.

3 Stitch the squares together in 3 rows.

2 Assemble each of the 9 smaller squares or patches.

4 Join the rows to complete the block.

BLOCKS

SQUARES AND RECTANGLES

A surprising number of very attractive blocks can be made up purely out of squares and rectangles — and of course the straightforward angles of seams make these blocks very easy to stitch! Draw the block up carefully on graph paper so that you can cut your templates accurately.

POPULAR SQUARE AND RECTANGLE BLOCKS

Chequerboard	*Checks or Bricks*	*Turned Rectangles*
Going Down Stairs	*Brick Wall*	*Up and Down*
Strip Pattern	*Zigzag Bricks*	*Roman Squares*

LEFT This quilt design is known as Double Irish Chain, and is a clever mixture of pieced blocks, and plain blocks with small squares appliquéd to them to build up the chain pattern. The pieced blocks are 5 × 5 chequerboard squares, and the blocks in between are plain with a square appliquéd in each corner.

LEFT Bricks is the appropriate name for the pattern used in this early American quilt design.

BLOCKS

TRIANGLES

As with English patchwork, triangles in American patchwork are surprisingly versatile for such simple shapes. Triangles of the same size or of different sizes can be combined into many different block designs, and the ways that the colours and fabrics can be arranged bring yet more possibilities into the designs.

POSITIONING TRIANGLE BLOCKS

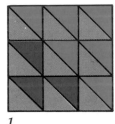

1

2

3

Even simple triangle blocks can be built up into very complex designs if you plan your project out carefully beforehand. Draw your design up on squared paper, and work out what colours the different triangles should be. The example here shows a basic three-colour block built up into an intricate quilt design.

1 A single block made up of 6 light, 3 medium and 9 dark triangles.
2 4 blocks stitched together.
3 A group of 16 similar blocks joined into a larger pattern.

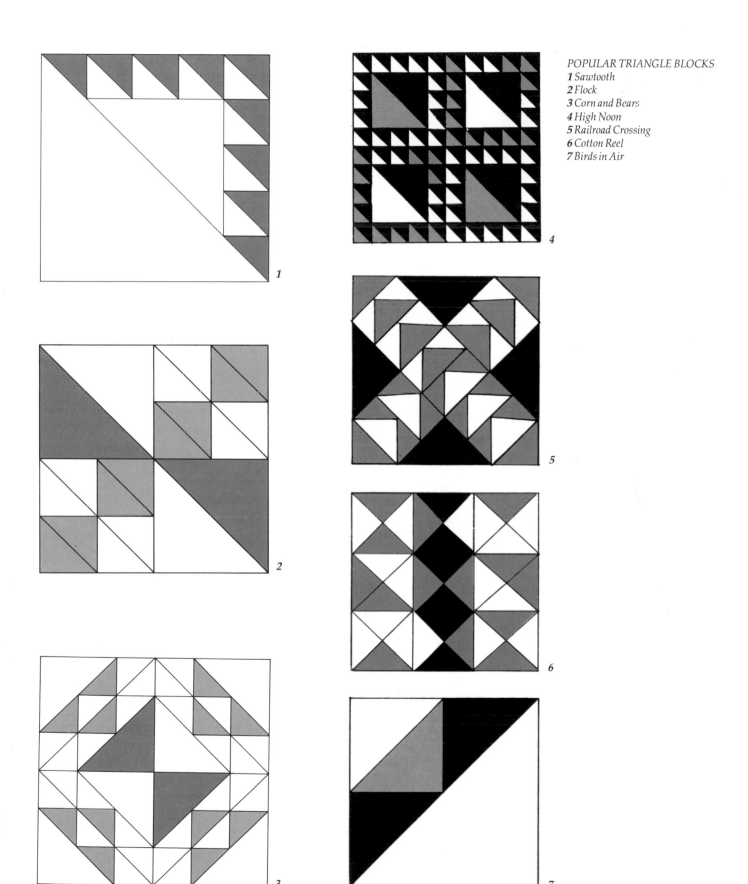

POPULAR TRIANGLE BLOCKS
1 Sawtooth
2 Flock
3 Corn and Bears
4 High Noon
5 Railroad Crossing
6 Cotton Reel
7 Birds in Air

BLOCKS

SQUARES AND TRIANGLES

Some of the most popular block designs are made up from a combination of squares and triangles. Even though some of these look very intricate, they are quite straightforward to make as long as you carefully assemble the small patches first before joining them into the full-size blocks.

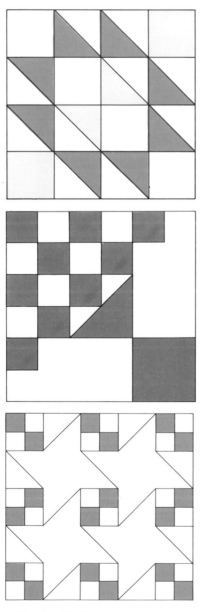

Hovering Hawks
Steps to the Altar
Milky Way

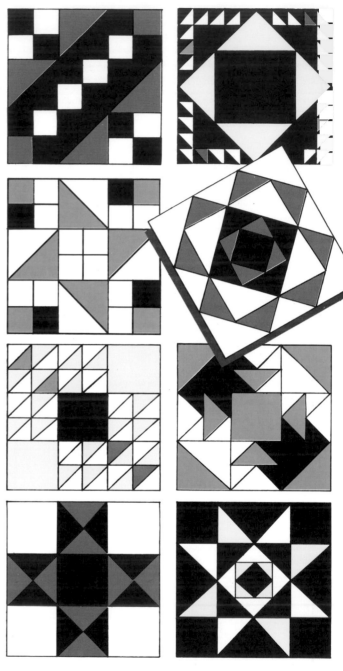

Jacob's Ladder
Water Wheel
Winged Square
Ohio Star

Shark's Tooth Square
Double T
Handy Andy
Boxed Square

Rising Star
Eight Hand Round
Lemoyne Star
54-40

Greek Cross
Flying Dutchman
Tall Pine Tree
Weather Vane

Red Cross
Goose in the Pond
Sherman's March
Rolling Stone

BLOCKS

ORNATE DESIGNS

Once you have mastered the basic art of making blocks with American patchwork, you can easily translate your skill to more complex block designs. All you need to do is use the same basic principles as you

do for the easier blocks; draw your pattern up carefully, work out the piecing order, and stitch your seams accurately.

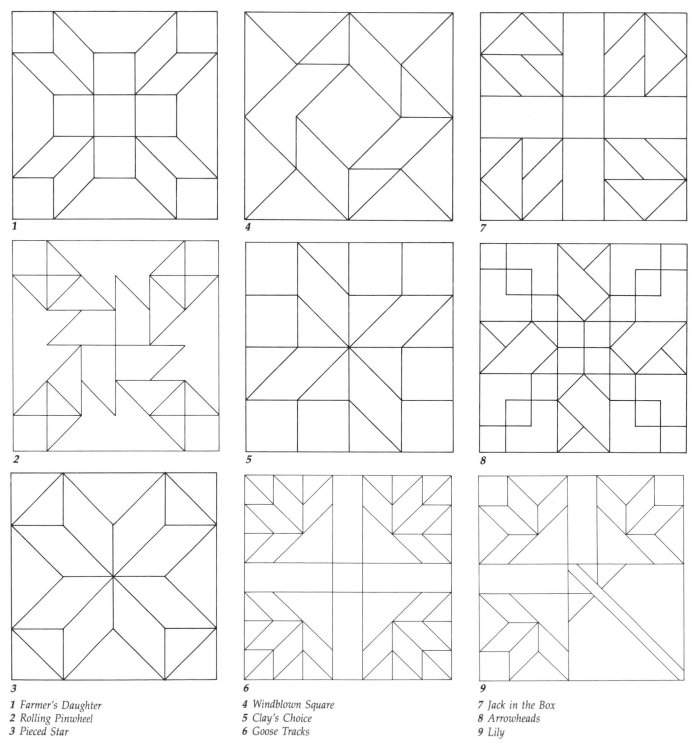

1 Farmer's Daughter
2 Rolling Pinwheel
3 Pieced Star

4 Windblown Square
5 Clay's Choice
6 Goose Tracks

7 Jack in the Box
8 Arrowheads
9 Lily

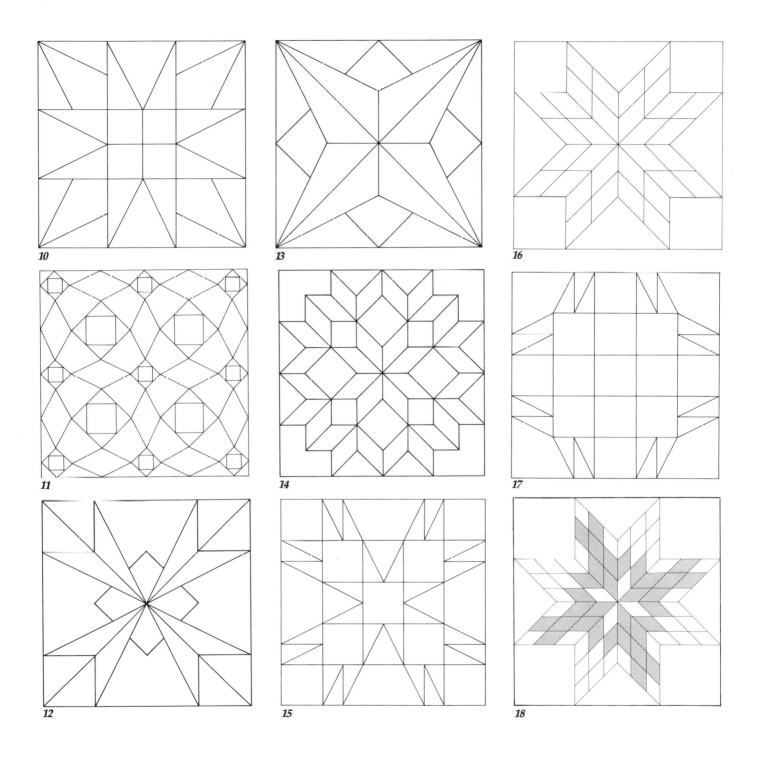

10 Claws
11 Storm at Sea
12 Double Star

13 Star
14 Dutch Rose
15 St Louis Star

16 Eastern Star
17 Pigeon Toes
18 Dove in the Window

BLOCKS

COMBINING BLOCKS

As your confidence with piecing blocks grows, you can plan projects which exploit the secondary patterns that are produced when several blocks are stitched together. The shapes and colours of the blocks flow into one another, creating new lines of interest and larger patterns; you may want to plan your patchwork so that the colours grow lighter, darker or brighter across the project, or so that there is a focal point of colour or pattern.

RIGHT Album quilts are made up of different patterned blocks bordered with lattice strips, or sashing. Quilts like these are ideal for practising different block designs, or for group work where everyone can piece a different block, perhaps in the same fabrics.

RIGHT Several Fruit Basket blocks are combined in this quilt, called November Morning. Some of the patches have been worked with the background fabric, and some of the cut patches of fabric have been appliquéd to the quilt outside the joined blocks, giving the impression of an unfinished jigsaw.

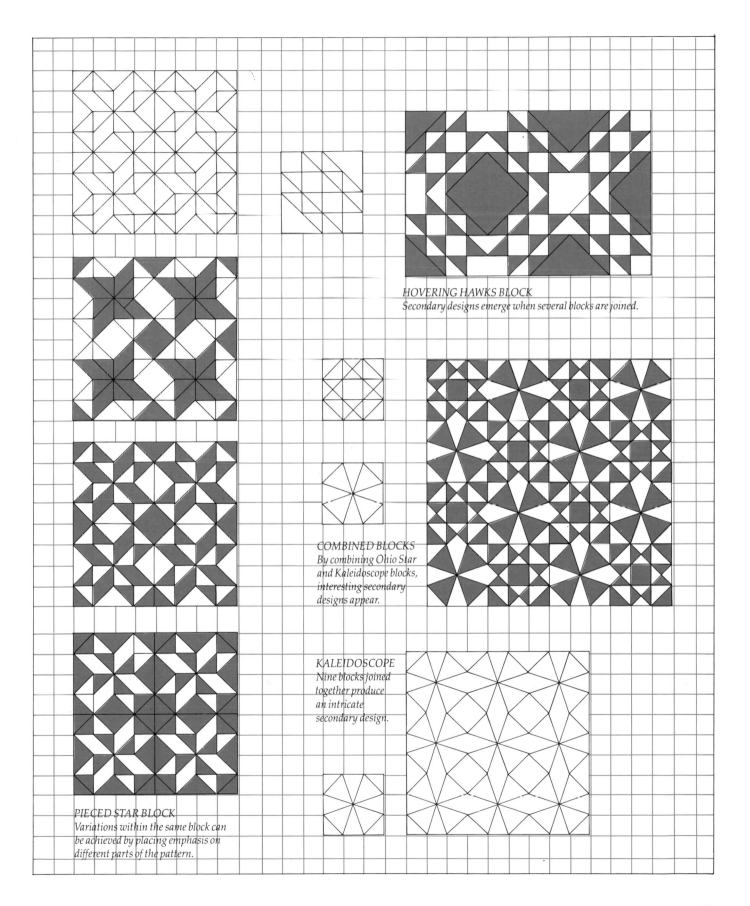

HOVERING HAWKS BLOCK
Secondary designs emerge when several blocks are joined.

COMBINED BLOCKS
By combining Ohio Star
and Kaleidoscope blocks,
interesting secondary
designs appear.

KALEIDOSCOPE
Nine blocks joined
together produce
an intricate
secondary design.

PIECED STAR BLOCK
Variations within the same block can
be achieved by placing emphasis on
different parts of the pattern.

SEMINOLE PATCHWORK

METHOD

This form of strip patchwork developed by the Seminole Indians uses thin strips of coloured fabrics which are first stitched together, cut up and then rearranged into brilliant coloured patterns — often with tiny mosaic-like patches much smaller in size than in ordinary patchwork.

The development of this simple, yet ingenious method of creating complex-looking designs was directly influenced by the introduction of the sewing machine. Closely-woven cottons or silks in plain, primary or subtle colours work well but patterned fabrics should be chosen with care. Certain patterns do not always give the right amount of contrast and the finished effect may be disappointing. Also, since there are so many seems involved, heavier fabrics are best avoided. These would be bulky and unattractive. Although the width of the strips can be varied, more intricate effects are achieved with narrower strips, but they should not be less than 2cm (³/₄in), including seams.

The small-scale effect of the patchwork makes it ideal for children's clothes — inserted dress panels and borders, for example; shirt yokes, pockets, bags, cushions and wall hangings.

Either make a scaled plan of your design, or, if you are not sure how your shapes will work out,

experiment, using fabric oddments, by cutting and stitching several different strip patterns to find the most pleasing arrangements, and then plan your design.

BELOW Striking geometric patterns can be produced with very simple Seminole patchwork, as this small quilt shows.

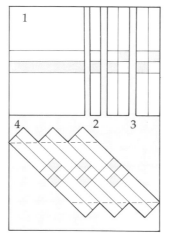

STRAIGHT-CUT STRIPS
1 Sew together a selection of strips (always cut on the straight grain) — four in this case.
2 Then cut them into equal strips.
3 Reverse and join the strips together in pairs.
4 Stitch the pairs in a diagonal position. This offsets the four patch squares to give a row of diamonds. Trim the top and bottom level ready to join on the next plain or patterned band.

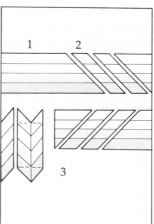

BIAS-CUT STRIPS
1 Sew together two coloured strips — cut on the straight grain and slightly wider than before.
2 Cut them diagonally into even sections.
3 Reposition and stitch the strips diagonally matching the corner points. Trim off the top and bottom, as shown, to give a border of triangles.

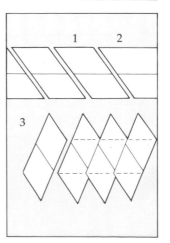

CHEVRONS
1 Sew together the required number of coloured strips.
2 Cut the length in half, and then cut each one into even sections cutting diagonally in the opposite direction.
3 With the bias edges and right sides together, join opposite pieces. Continue in this way, adding more chevrons as needed. Press and trim the edges.

ABOVE AND LEFT Modern interpretations of Seminole patchwork can produce some beautiful designs, like this carefully pieced cushion cover. The diagram shows how the sections of Seminole patchwork were cut and positioned to produce the pattern.

SEMINOLE PATCHWORK

MODERN PATTERNS

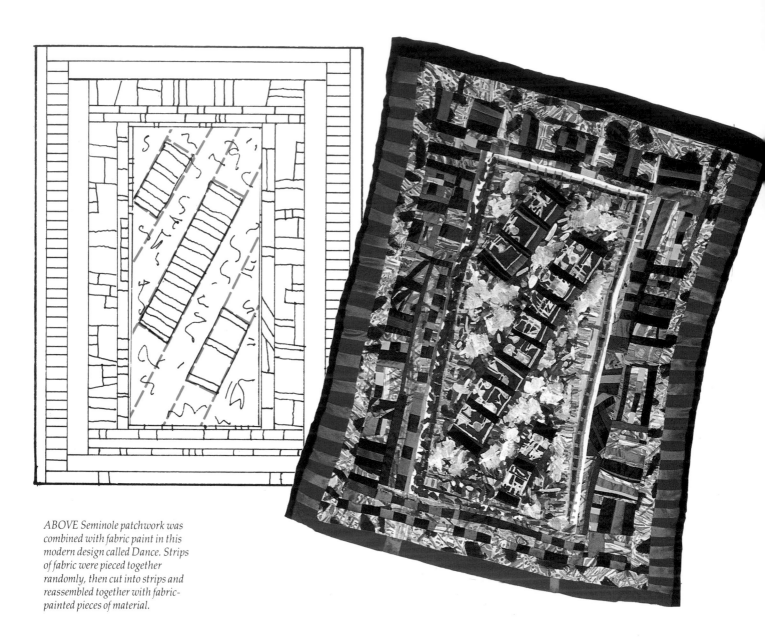

ABOVE Seminole patchwork was
combined with fabric paint in this
modern design called Dance. Strips
of fabric were pieced together
randomly, then cut into strips and
reassembled together with fabric-
painted pieces of material.

RIGHT Dazzling, eye-catching designs are a special feature of Seminole
patchwork. Many geometric patterns designed to create optical illusions
translate well into this type of patchwork. Several colours can be used for more
complex effects, or just two strongly contrasting tones, as in this amazing
contemporary quilt.

Here blocks of black and white checks are cut and repositioned to create a
third illusory dimension of swirling movement. Fine- to lightweight cotton or
cotton mixtures are excellent for designs where so many seams are involved.
In order fully to appreciate the effect, optical designs usually require a fairly
large expanse, such as quilts, covers, duvets and rugs. However, four blocks
would make a handsome floor cushion or bolster, or a smaller wall hanging.

STRIP PATCHWORK

Strip Patchwork involves stitching together long strips of fabric in patterns. This is one of the easiest methods of making patchwork. Templates are not used and the whole patchwork can be quickly stitched by machine without a foundation fabric. Strips can either be joined and quilted in one operation, or quilted in the usual way as for wadded quilting.

Simple strip designs can be adapted quite imaginatively for floor rugs, sleeping bags, crib or cot covers and play mats. Made up and quilted without a wadded interlining, strip patchwork makes stunning duvet and pillow covers — teaming the colours but varying the stripes. Any fabric can be used from wool, tweeds and suitings (for rugs) to silks, satins, cottons, cotton/wool mixes, velvets and corduroys.

ABOVE Alphabet fabric was the perfect choice for a nursery quilt made from strips of different widths.

STITCHING METHOD

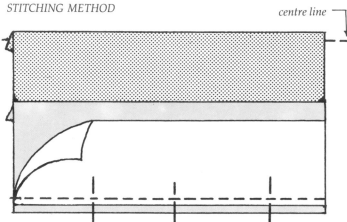

Starting in the middle of the quilt, apply the strips for the first half. Turn the work round and complete the second half working in the same way, taking care to place any motifs or letters the correct way up.

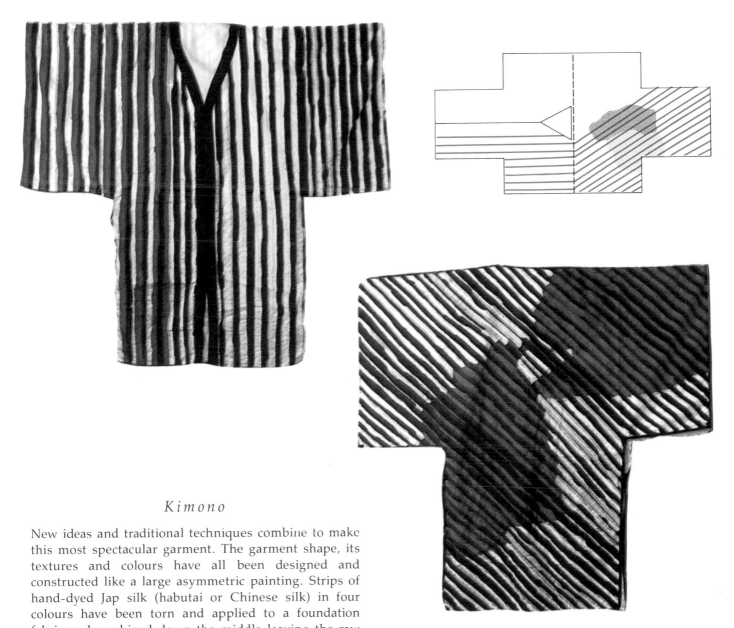

Kimono

New ideas and traditional techniques combine to make this most spectacular garment. The garment shape, its textures and colours have all been designed and constructed like a large asymmetric painting. Strips of hand-dyed Jap silk (habutai or Chinese silk) in four colours have been torn and applied to a foundation fabric and machined down the middle leaving the raw edges to fray and give a slightly furry effect to the entire surface.

The technique works equally well with other fabrics such as loosely woven cottons, linens, taffetas and certain wools and tweeds. Similar patchwork made from softer fabrics is extremely comfortable to wear and is ideal for all kinds of garments, from amazing evening coats and wraps to part-decorated silk T-shirts. Heavier fabrics are best for floor or wall coverings and chunky-style cushions.

Make a scale drawing of your design with colour suggestions. Collect suitable fabrics together (dye fine silk with commercial cold-water dyes) and prepare the strips, tearing them across the fabric in mixed widths between 2-3cm ($\frac{3}{4}$-$1\frac{1}{4}$in). Draw the outline of the garment on the backing fabric — a medium-weight polyester/cotton provides the right amount of firmness and stability to the silk. Check your own measurements against the outline from a loose-fitting garment or a commercial pattern. Using matching coloured threads throughout, stitch evenly spaced black strips, first folding the strip at the shoulder to change its direction. Then add the remaining strips between, overlapping the ends where the colours meet. Cut out the garment and line with fine silk. Bind around the edges to finish.

LOG CABIN

INTRODUCTION

Log Cabin (or Canadian Patchwork) is a famous American design using contrasting light and darker strips of fabric, which represent the construction of the north American log cabins. The same design is also found in Britain, other European countries, the Middle East and Afghanistan.

The narrow strips of varying lengths are stitched on to a square of foundation fabric to make 'pressed' rather than pieced blocks. Starting from the middle, a small square, the 'fire' or 'hearth', is stitched down and then the foundation is covered with the light and darker strips of fabric, each strip in turn being stitched, turned back to the right side and pressed as the work progresses — the light and dark sides of the block representing firelight and shadows.

STITCHING SEQUENCES

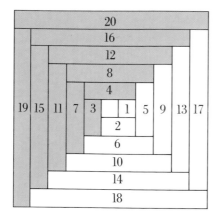

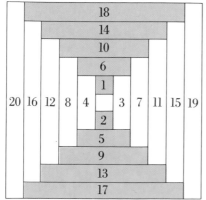

The diagrams show the stitching sequences for the light and dark fabrics for the basic Log Cabin block, and one of the popular variations.

1 Log Cabin
2 Courthouse Steps
Note that on the Log Cabin block the strips are sewn on in a spiral sequence, while in Courthouse Steps they are stitched down either side of the central square each time.

The advantage of this design is that all kinds of leftover scraps can be put to good use. Traditionally, dress and shirt cottons, wool, worsted and tweeds were used. Later, the Victorians used shiny silk and satin ribbons transforming the finished effect from a homespun textile born of thrift and ingenuity into a smart, multi-coloured fabric. While all cottons are easy to handle and thoroughly reliable for patchwork, other contemporary fabrics offer a fantastic range of textures and finishes to experiment with, including novelty synthetics, sheer metallic fabrics and a vast choice of ribbons. Plaids, spots, checks, flecks, stripes and many other patterns may all be used to give new optical effects.

Log Cabin Designs

Using the basic square, an amazing variety of patterns can be constructed, depending on how the light and dark sections are arranged within the block, and on how the blocks are finally put together. In America each part has its own name; Log Cabin, Courthouse Steps and Pineapple, for example, are three variations of the individual block while Straight Furrow, Stepping Stones, Flight of Stairs, Barn Raising and Chequerboard are names of the arrangements.

The patchwork is not usually bordered but it should be lined and top stitched between the seams of the blocks. A 30cm (12in) square block is a popular size for making quilts and 15cm (6in) square for cushions or smaller projects. The strips are usually 2.5cm (1in) wide plus 6mm ($\frac{1}{4}$in) seam allowances, but, on fine fabrics, they may be cut twice the width and used double. You will need equal amounts of light and dark fabrics for the patchwork, plus foundation and lining fabric the size of the project, excluding seam allowances.

Log Cabin is eminently suitable for cushions, using one large or four smaller blocks, crib covers with 12 smaller blocks, cot quilts, full-size quilts and wall hangings.

RIGHT Once Log Cabin blocks have been pieced, they can be stitched together to form secondary patterns through their arrangements of light and dark tones.

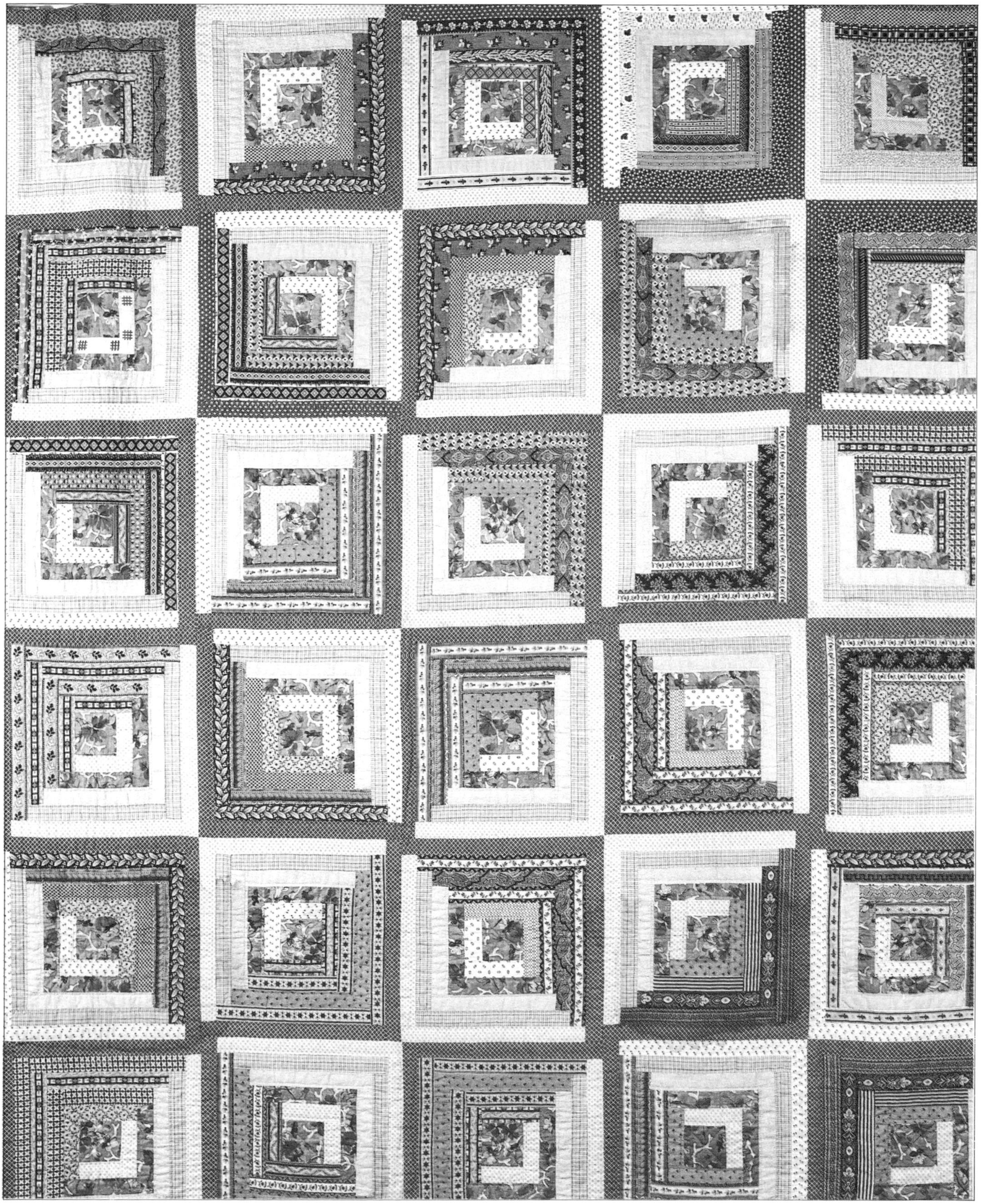

LOG CABIN

METHOD

The Log Cabin is an ideal design for a scrap quilt, so a good collection of fabrics in pure cotton or polycotton is necessary. If you are buying new fabrics, eleven different ones are needed for a basic block, five in light and five in dark tones and one for the centre square. In traditional patterns the centre square is often red, to represent the log fire in the cabin, but for modern Log Cabin you can choose any colour.

Preparation

Sort fabrics into light and dark values; plain or patterned fabrics can be used, or a combination of the two. The important point is to have two contrasting groups of fabrics.

Cut the strips on the straight grain of the fabric either lengthwise or crosswise. Mark the strips by drawing directly onto the fabric with a fabric marker. If you are using new fabric a rotary cutter and board will speed up cutting. Cut the strips accurately, as any inaccuracy in cutting out will transfer itself to the stitching, and then to the finished blocks; it will create blocks of unequal sizes, and cause difficulty in fitting them together, resulting ultimately in unevenness in the appearance of the overall quilt design.

For a 41cm (16in) block made up of five rounds of strips, the finished size of the centre square needs to be 9cm (3½in) across, and the strips need to be 32mm (1¼in) wide, so add 6mm (¼in) seam allowance all round when cutting out. Cut fabric for the centre

RIGHT A Log Cabin quilt in pretty floral fabrics gives a lovely country cottage effect in a guest-room.

square 10cm × 10cm (4in × 4in) and the strips 4.5cm (1¾in) wide. This block can be made by hand or machine; a running stitch 6mm (¼in) from the cut edge is used to stitch fabrics together. Make sure that you stitch the seams very straight, and an even distance from the edge in every seam.

Making up the Blocks

Cut the centre squares; they should measure 10cm × 10cm (4in × 4in). Then select the fabric to be used for the first strip. Cut a length to fit the side of the square and pin right sides together. Stitch 6mm (¼in) from the edge. On the wrong side press the seam towards the strip. Using the same fabric for strip 2, cut another

length to fit the edge of the square plus the added width of strip 1. Pin, stitch and press as before.

The third and fourth strips are cut from the contrasting tone-value group. Cut strip 3 the length of the square plus the edge of strip 2; pin, stitch and press. The fourth strip completes the first round.

Continue adding strips, increasing the length of each to accommodate the width of the previous strip, and placing light and dark fabrics in the correct sequence. The strips can rotate in a clockwise or anti-clockwise direction, but must be consistent in all blocks and not change direction. This will ensure that your final project looks regular when the blocks are joined into a pattern.

STITCHING A LOG CABIN BLOCK

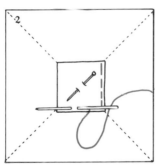

1 Cut a square of backing fabric to size plus 15mm (½in) seam allowances all round. Mark it diagonally both ways either by tacking stitches or with a light pencil line. Pin a 5cm (2in) square in the middle and secure with small running stitches, or by machine.

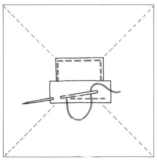

2 Cut a light strip 6mm (¼in) longer at each end than the central square by 6.5cm (2½in) wide, and fold lengthways in half. With right sides together, place the fold over the edge of the central square and stitch across.

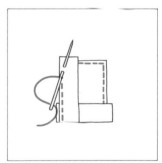

3 Press the strip back to the right side. Apply a second light strip 6mm (¼in) longer at each end than the length of the central square and strip, stitch and press back.

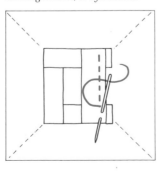

4 Apply dark strips in the same way working around the square, stitching and pressing them back to the right side.

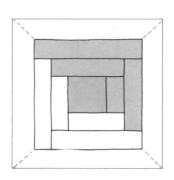

5 Repeat the sequence adding light and dark strips to complete the block.

LOG CABIN

TRADITIONAL VARIATIONS

STRAIGHT FURROW
ABOVE AND RIGHT The two examples here show the pattern called Straight Furrow; the blocks are arranged so that the light and dark corners form diagonal furrows of light and dark fabrics across the quilt.

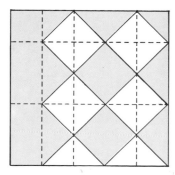

BARN RAISING
LEFT Barn Raising is a variation of
Straight Furrow; in Barn Raising the
furrows are arranged so that they
form an overall diamond pattern
across the quilt as a whole. On this
example an elaborate border has been
formed from separately pieced blocks.

STARRY NIGHT
BELOW In the pattern Starry Night,
blocks are arranged in groups of four
with the light corners all at the centre
of the arrangement. When these
groups of four blocks are in turn
joined, an overall pattern of light and
dark star shapes is formed. The detail
and illustration show the 'all-dark'
border; blocks have been made using
dark fabrics all the way round
instead of alternating them with
light fabrics.

LOG CABIN

MODERN VARIATIONS

CRAZY LOG
Crazy Log is a modern, random version of Log Cabin. Instead of using neat central squares and uniform-width strips, irregular rectangles are used in the centres of the blocks and surrounded with random strips of different fabrics in different widths and set at varying angles. The traditional light and dark variations are ignored.

Once you are good at doing neat Log Cabin blocks, it can be quite difficult to make yourself sew the strips on crooked deliberately! You will soon get the knack, though, and will discover that Crazy Log can be great fun.

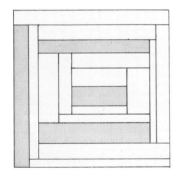

ABOVE A typical example of a Crazy Log block.

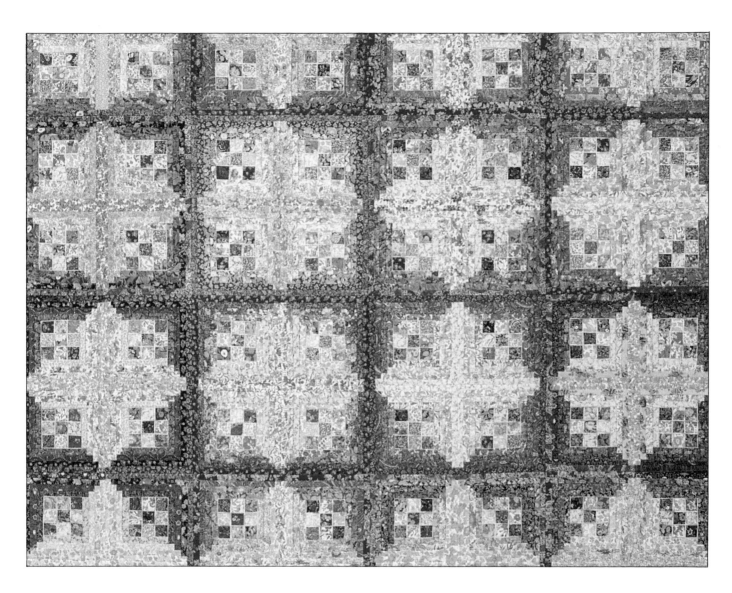

LOG CABIN WINDOWS

This quilt is a contemporary interpretation of the traditional Log Cabin block, set in the 'light and dark' or 'sunshine and shadow' variation. Each set of four blocks has the lighter sides set together making strong, light diamonds. The red fabrics used on the dark sides of the centre blocks are carried half-way into the edging and corner blocks. The block centres are not a plain square, but a tiny nine-patch of floral fabric embroidered with satin stitch in a multi-coloured thread.

The 'logs' or strips of each block are folded and applied to a base fabric giving the quilt added surface texture. This is a development of the technique used in some old Log Cabin quilts where the pieced fabric was stitched onto squares of backing, thereby dispensing with the need for a filler. Once the quilt top is completed all that is needed is a backing sheet to conceal the seams. This folding and stitching makes a rather heavy quilt which is therefore more suitable for a wall hanging or throw than for use as a bedspread.

RIGHT The detailed photograph shows the pleated strips stitched round the central panelled square.

DIAMOND LOG CABIN

INTRODUCTION

The Blazing Star design was one favoured by the expert needlewoman to show off her skills in a masterpiece quilt, and the graphic qualities of this design are added to those of the Log Cabin by altering the shape of the block centres in this quilt. The blocks are constructed in the same way as the square Log Cabin, with strips rotating around a central piece, but the central piece is a diamond rather than a square.

The same principles of light and shade manipulation are used to dynamic effect. When the blocks are set together in a large six-pointed star, with the dark sides of the block innermost, a pattern of radiating hexagons emerges. The red diamond centres of each of the fifty-four blocks pivot the eye around the star shape.

The possible problem of fitting this shape into a final frame has been solved by making the quilt a large hexagon, filling the negative space with six plain diamonds which reflect each segment of the centre star. A striped border of darker fabrics edges the quilt. The centre star shape is tied rather than quilted so there is no surface stitching to detract from the central pattern, whilst the outer diamonds are closely quilted by machine. The size of the quilt is approximately 260cm (100in) wide.

Making up the Blocks

Trace the centre template and cut out the diamond centres in your chosen fabric. The finished width of the strips is 13mm ($\frac{1}{2}$in) so cut them 25mm (1in) wide to allow 6mm ($\frac{1}{4}$in) seam allowance each side. The first two strips are light coloured. Lay a strip along one side of the diamond centre with the right sides together, leaving enough fabric each end to trim to the correct angle after stitching. Stitch, taking in a 6mm ($\frac{1}{4}$in) seam allowance. On the wrong side press the seam towards the diamond centre and trim the ends of the strip in line with the sides of the diamond, maintaining the correct angle. Add strip 2 in the same light fabric, stitch, press and trim as before.

Strips 3 and 4 are dark coloured. Add the third strip stitching, pressing and trimming as before.

Strip 4 completes the first round of strips. Continue to add strips keeping the light and dark fabrics in sequence until four rounds have been completed. Fifty-four Diamond Log Cabin blocks are required for the six-pointed star.

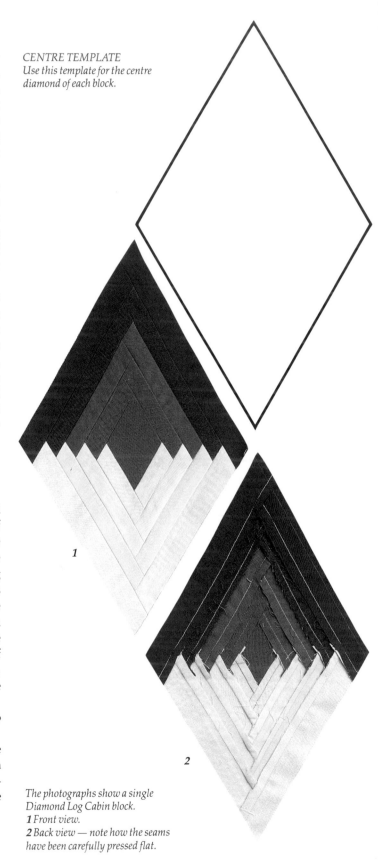

CENTRE TEMPLATE
Use this template for the centre diamond of each block.

1

2

The photographs show a single Diamond Log Cabin block.
1 Front view.
2 Back view — note how the seams have been carefully pressed flat.

ABOVE This Blazing Star quilt was stitched by machine in the Diamond Log Cabin design, then quilted around the plain diamonds.

DIAMOND LOG CABIN

METHOD

PIECING ORDER
1 *Allow extra fabric at the ends of the strips to give room for trimming. Stitch the first strip to the diamond, working with the diamond on top so that you know where to begin and finish stitching.*
2 *Press the strip away from the diamond and trim the ends, extending the angle of the sides of the central diamond.*
3 *Attach the second strip to the next side in the same way.*
4 *Press the second strip over and trim in the same way as for the first strip.*
5 *Change to a dark-toned fabric and use this for the third strip; attach it to the third side of the diamond.*
6 *Press the third strip over and trim it in the same way.*
7 *Use the dark fabric to add the fourth strip, which is the final strip in the first round.*
8 *Press the fourth strip over and trim; you now have a frame around the central diamond. Add the next rounds of strips in the same way, beginning always with the same side of the diamond and working round in a spiral.*

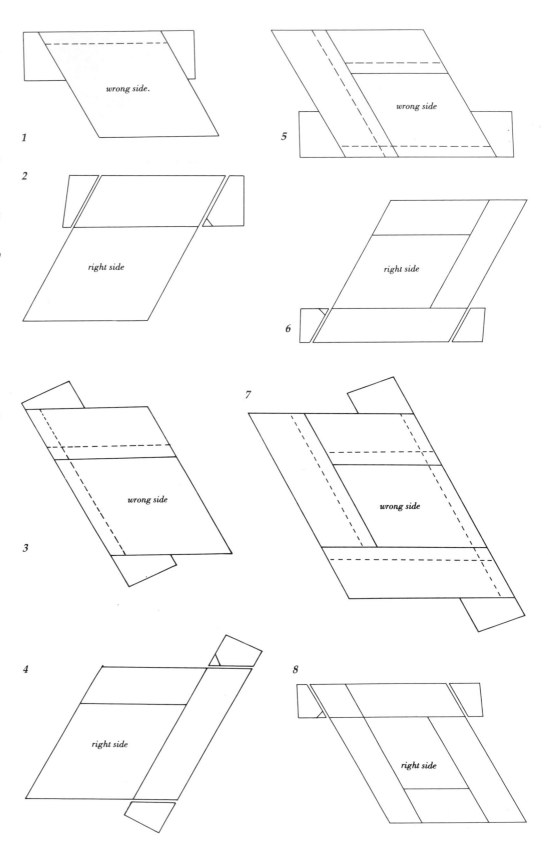

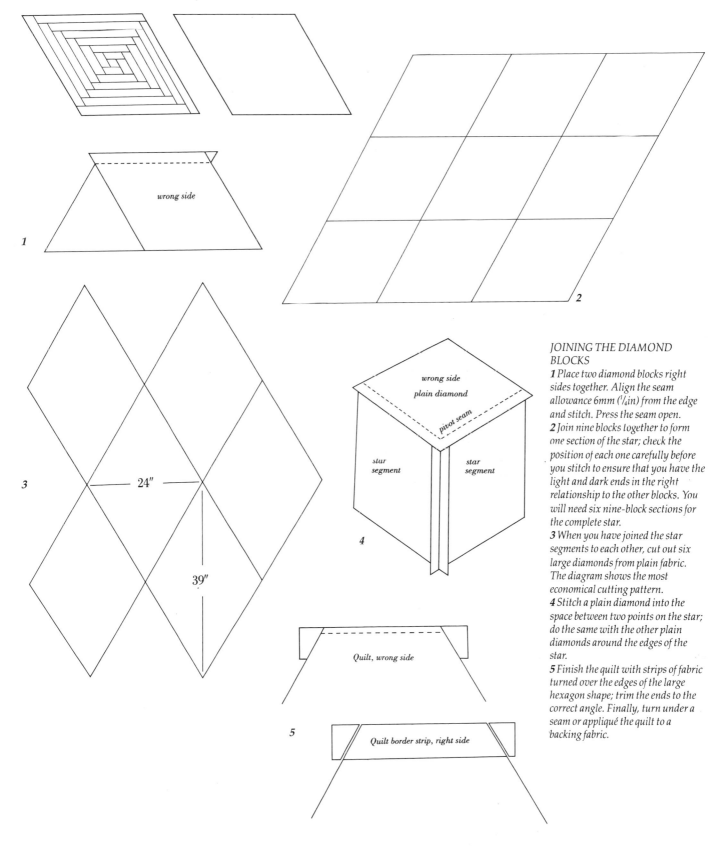

1

wrong side

2

3

24″

39″

4

wrong side
plain diamond
pivot seam

star segment

star segment

5

Quilt, wrong side

Quilt border strip, right side

JOINING THE DIAMOND BLOCKS

1 Place two diamond blocks right sides together. Align the seam allowance 6mm (¼in) from the edge and stitch. Press the seam open.

2 Join nine blocks together to form one section of the star; check the position of each one carefully before you stitch to ensure that you have the light and dark ends in the right relationship to the other blocks. You will need six nine-block sections for the complete star.

3 When you have joined the star segments to each other, cut out six large diamonds from plain fabric. The diagram shows the most economical cutting pattern.

4 Stitch a plain diamond into the space between two points on the star; do the same with the other plain diamonds around the edges of the star.

5 Finish the quilt with strips of fabric turned over the edges of the large hexagon shape; trim the ends to the correct angle. Finally, turn under a seam or appliqué the quilt to a backing fabric.

PLEATED PATCHWORK

PLEATS AND TUCKS

As its name suggests, pleated patchwork involves joining together blocks of pleated fabric arranged to give interesting textural and optical effects. This purely decorative patchwork, in which the surface texture of the fabric is deliberately altered before the blocks are joined, offers great scope for innovation.

Regularly formed pleats are machine stitched and can either be stitched down at each side of a block, following the direction of the folds to give a softly ridged surface, or additional lines may also be stitched diagonally across, or at right angles to the first set of folds. This alters the surface tension, and, in this way, the play of light creates quite amazing effects of movement reminiscent of drifting sand dunes.

Pin tucks can also be used. These are usually stitched quite near the folded edge of the fabric, although the depth can be varied as needed. They can be stitched in sequence either vertically or horizontally, or in both directions to form a chequered pattern. The same stitching can be used throughout, or in different sequences of straight stitch and satin stitch worked over the edge in matching, contrast or variegated coloured threads. Pin tucks combined with pleating and 'movement stitching' offer a whole new range of visual effects.

The prepared fabric is then cut into the correct size blocks and arranged to suit the design. Rectangular blocks can be joined together either following a simple square grid, in vertical or horizontal bands across, or cut into block-size geometric shapes such as triangles, parallelograms and diamonds, for example, before being stitched in pattern.

As most of the interest in pleated patchwork relies on the undulating surfaces created and the way in which the blocks are put together, plain, pastel coloured fabrics will give best results. Voile, cotton, cotton/polyester, silk, gingham, fine velvet, chiffon, lace and certain nets are ideal. However, simple, spotted, striped and shaded fabrics might also be exploited. By obscuring and distorting the design with pleats and tucks, areas of solid colour, or increased density of pattern, can be produced and used in imaginative piecing. The finished work should be lined to hide the seaming.

Pleats

Pleating and tucking reduces the fabric depending on the depth of the folds used. For full pleating, allow at least three times the finished size.

As an alternative to using regularly spaced pleats of an equal size throughout a patchwork, you can ring the changes by mixing areas of both deep and shallower pleats in a design. This will give a more undulating and sculptural effect to the surface, which can also be further emphasised by stitching with shaded threads. Take extra care when estimating the amount of fabric needed.

Tucks

For a combined effect of tucks and pleats stitch the pleats as far as setting the folds, as previously described, and then stitch the creased lines as described for tucks. Use matching or contrast colours, changing them to emphasise the effects of movement.

MAKING PLEATS

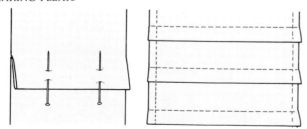

1 Decide the depth of the pleat — 15mm (¹/₂in) is a popular size. Working on the right side, and along the straight grain of the fabric, pin the first fold across and press.
2 For the next and subsequent pleats, release the first fold, measure the depth and the distance between and then, using pins, mark the foldlines and positioning lines along both edges. Complete each pleat stitching 15mm (¹/₂in) in from the edge. Press and stitch the pleats down each side in the direction of the folds.

MAKING TUCKS

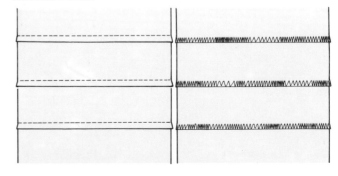

1 To make simple tucks, fold the fabric along the straight grain and, using matching or contrast coloured threads, machine between 3-6mm (¹/₈-¹/₄in) in from the edge. Press the tuck to one side and repeat as needed. Accurate straight stitching is essential.
2 Alternatively, zigzag stitch the edges, using a variegated thread.

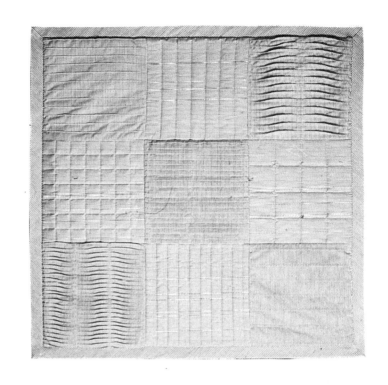

Being much finer than pleats, tucks can be stitched quite close together over an entire area in regular or random designs, to give a gently ridged surface. They can also be spaced apart and worked in both directions to produce checks, and with a little more effort, checks can be varied to create a tartan effect. As with pleats, take care in estimating the amount of fabric needed, remembering with tartan-type designs, to calculate both directions accurately.

RIGHT AND BELOW Despite the geometric constrictions involved in pleating and tucking, softly textured and surprisingly free-flowing patterns can be achieved, as shown by this delightful contemporary quilt. Made from striped cotton ticking, it combines quilting with pleating and tucking in a very simple way. Blocks of vertical quilting are pieced alternately with blocks of horizontal folding to suggest a large basketweave pattern. The quilt is finished with a 5cm (2in) wide bias-cut border where the diagonal stripes of the ticking make an interesting contrast. The close-up photograph shows the pattern in which the pleats have been stitched down.

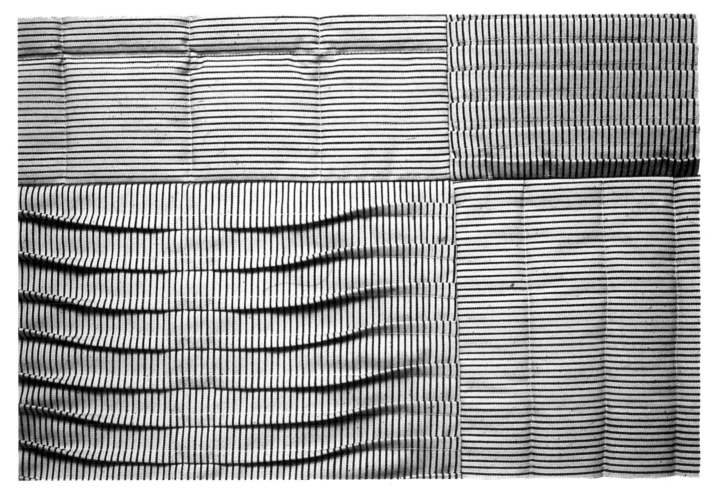

PLEATED PATCHWORK

TECHNIQUES

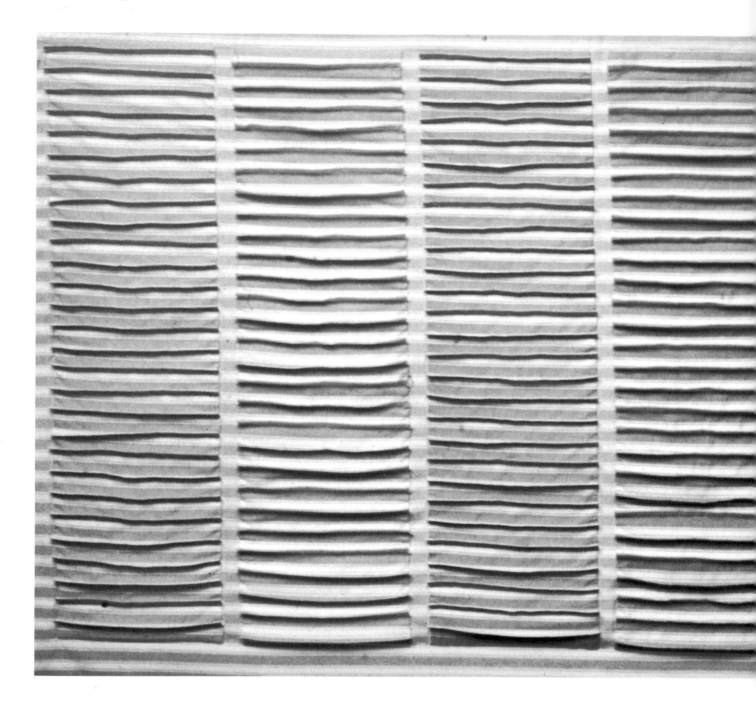

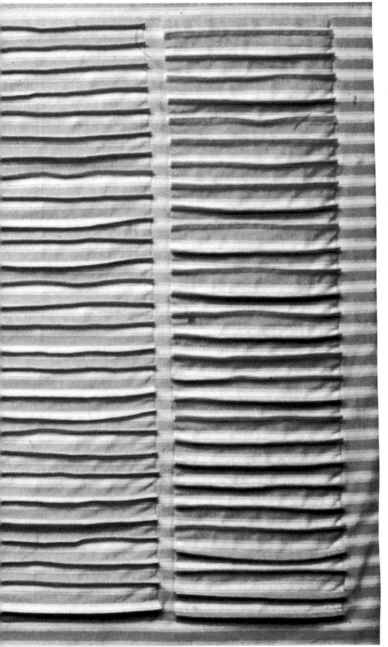

MOVEMENT STITCHING

For 'movement stitching' either machine the outer edges of a block with the folds in opposite directions, or repeat over the entire surface stitching the folds up and down, or diagonally, in alternate directions. Hold the fabric with both hands as you feed it through the machine, using pins as a guideline for stitching.

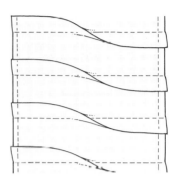

TUCKS AND PLEATS

For a combined effect of tucks and pleats stitch the pleats as far as setting the folds, as previously described, and then stitch the creased lines as described for tucks. Use matching or contrast colours, changing them to emphasise the effects of movement.

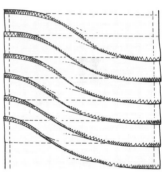

UPRIGHT PLEATS

Each fold is pinned in place and machine-stitched close to the lower crease line, first on one side then on the other. In this way, the double stitching helps to keep the fold in an upright position.

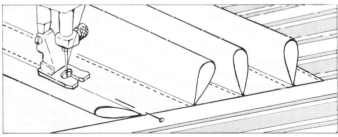

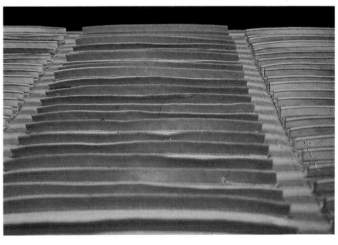

ABOVE AND RIGHT The pleats on this piece of patchwork have been stitched so that they stand upright, as the close-up photograph shows. Appropriately, this project is called Changing Colours.

FOLDED PATCHWORK

Folded Patchwork (sometimes called Quill patchwork) is made by attaching folded triangles of fabric (quills) to a ground fabric. The present technique, which was developed in Canada, is traditionally worked in patterns based on an eight-pointed star — one of the most popular motifs in American pieced patchwork.

Light- to medium-weight cottons that fold and crease well and are preferable to synthetics or silks which are too springy and slippery. Fabric oddments can be used, mixing patterns where necessary to give the correct tone rather than pattern. Small-scale prints, including flower sprigs, spots, checks, stripes and strong contrast plain colours, help to define the star motif. You will also need a foundation fabric which should not be too difficult to sew through — unbleached calico is ideal.

Building up the Star

A star pattern is built up by working outwards from the middle, overlapping triangles around a central point, and increasing the number in the rows as the patchwork is enlarged to the size required. The work naturally forms a circle but a design can easily be extended into a square. Each triangle needs a 5cm (2in) square of fabric, so, to get a rough idea of the overall amount needed, first make several practice triangles from fabric oddments or paper. Arrange them in pattern following the instructions, and then calculate the number of rows needed and the amounts of different fabrics for your planned design.

The finished patchwork block is the perfect shape for making cushion sets, or for piecing with alternate plain blocks, for example, into larger patchwork — and for lining the lids of laundry or sewing baskets. For a neat finish, borders and piped edges can be added, picking up the same or contrast colours, with a plain backing.

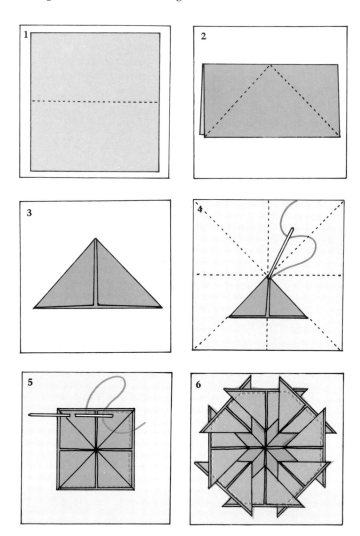

MAKING A FOUNDATION STAR
1 Cut out the correct number of 5cm (2in) squares from your chosen fabric. Fold in half.
2 Press flat. Make a triangle by folding the top corners to the centre of the base.
3 Make three more triangles in the same colour. Press the edges flat.
4 Mark the foundation fabric both ways through straight and diagonal centres. Pin the first triangle in place, and secure with a short straight stitch, as shown.
5 Attach three more triangles catching the centre points, and then secure the outer edges with running stitch through all layers 5mm (¼in) from the edge.
6 Add eight triangles in colour sequence placing the points about 1cm (½in) from the centre, overlapping the corners. Sew as before. Add eight more triangles on the next row placing the points between those of the last row, and continue in this way adding 16 on subsequent rows as the size increases, and so on, to finish your planned design.

ABOVE Folded patchwork lends itself very well to star patterns of all kinds; the one on this cushion cover is called Morning Star.

LEFT Tiny triangles of folded patchwork are used round the borders of the designs on this piece of South American needlework.

CATHEDRAL WINDOW

INTRODUCTION

Cathedral Window or Mayflower patchwork combines simple appliqué with folded patchwork. This ingenious technique is thought to have originated on the *Mayflower* carrying pilgrims to America, where the women used flour sacking to make the folded foundation blocks on which they stitched their precious pieces of printed and coloured fabrics in such a way as to be sparing (without making hems) and yet, give a bright overall effect of colourful patchwork.

Essentially, the work involves folding and refolding squares of the foundation fabric so that the finished patchwork is several layers thick and makes a light, warm covering suitable for throws. Also, as the outer edges are self-finishing, additional borders are not needed.

Choosing Fabrics

The method of preparing the foundation reduces the size of the original square by just over half, so allow about two and a quarter times the finished size for the foundation fabric. Although the squares may be larger or smaller, 15cm (6in) is a popular size. To help calculate the amount of fabric needed, a square this size will need a contrast square patch of about 5cm (2in).

Medium-weight cottons such as calico and poplin work well for the foundation and dressweight cottons for the patches. Plain fabrics inset with multi-coloured patches can look quite stunning and give dramatic cathedral window effects. Alternatively, multi-coloured backgrounds with plain patches can be equally attractive, reversing the effect to give a series of four-petalled flowers on a mixed ground.

Mayflower patchwork adapts well for cushions, bags, cot covers, quilts, throws and wall hangings.

PREPARING SQUARES BY HAND

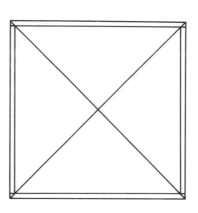

1

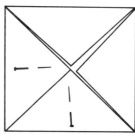

2

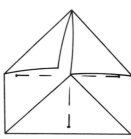

3

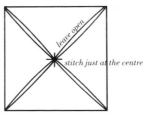

4

1 Turn a narrow hem on each square and press into place. Find the centre point of each square by folding and pressing diagonally.
2 Turn the corners to the centre point and pin in place; press to set the creases.
3 Fold the corners to the centre again.
4 Stitch across the centre to fasten the corners.

ABOVE By using striped fabric for the background, and rich little fragments of exotic silk, satin and velvet, the maker of this quilt has expoited the full potential of the technique. Folding and stitching has turned the black, purple and turquoise stripes in all directions, and the placing of the inserted pieces, concentrating the reds in the top corner, gives the impression of a glowing light through stained glass. Some of the panels are left unfilled, revealing the stripes, while others at the edge of the quilt sometimes stray into the border of narrow strips. These strips have been skilfully graduated through the tones, colours and textures of the fabrics round the quilt's edge.

CATHEDRAL WINDOW

STITCHING TECHNIQUES

PREPARING SQUARES BY MACHINE

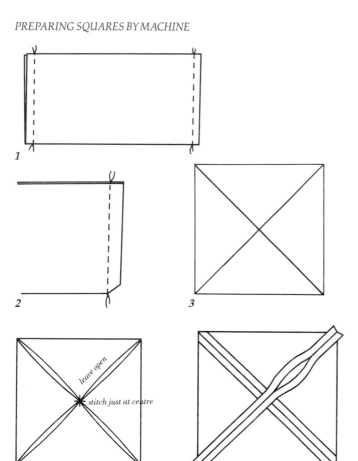

1

2

3

leave open

stitch just at centre

4

5

1 Fold the square in half and stitch up the sides, taking 6mm (¹/₄in) seam allowance.
2 Clip the corners of the seams on the folded side and press the seams open.
3 At the open side, place the seams together and stitch, leaving a gap to turn the square through to the right side.
4 Turn to the right side through the gap, poke the corners out, and press.
5 Fold the corners to the centre and stitch down at the centre only.

JOINING THE SQUARES

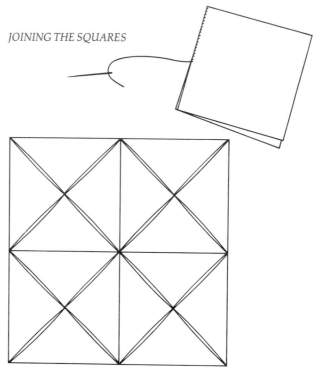

1 When you have prepared enough squares, place them right sides together and join along one edge from corner to corner with tiny oversewing stitches.
2 Join as many squares as you need for your design.

STITCHING IN THE DECORATIVE FABRICS

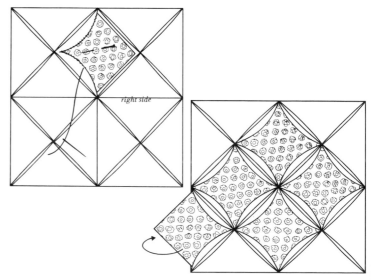

right side

1 Measure the space between two of the background squares and cut pieces of decorative fabric in that size. Turn the folded edge of the background over the decorative square and hem down neatly all round.
2 At the edges, hem the backing over two sides of the decorative square. Fold the remaining half of the decorative square to the back. Neaten the edges and hem down in place.

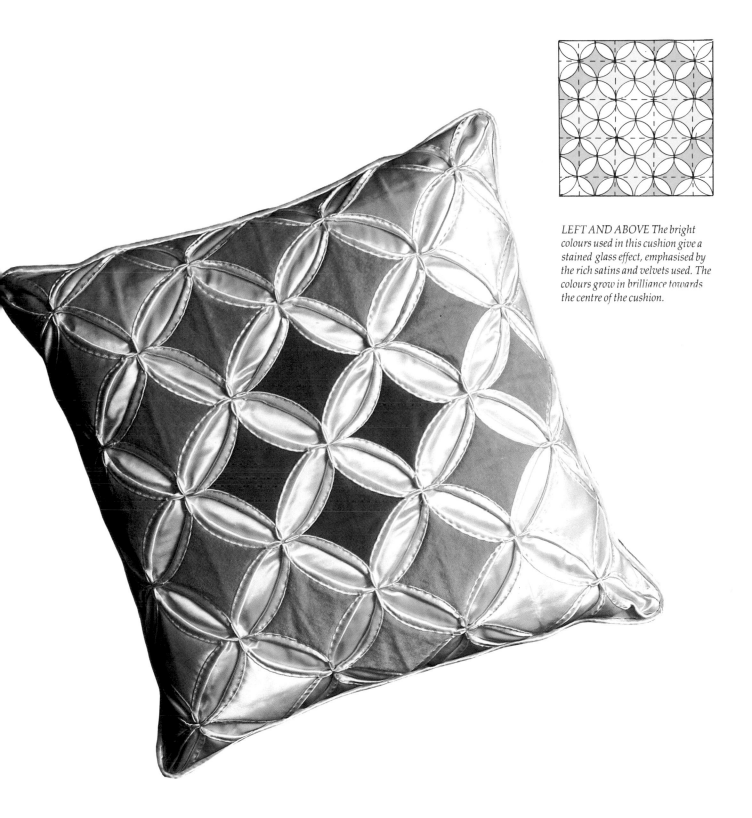

LEFT AND ABOVE The bright colours used in this cushion give a stained glass effect, emphasised by the rich satins and velvets used. The colours grow in brilliance towards the centre of the cushion.

ABSTRACT PANELS

You can make beautiful modern patchwork panels very easily with scraps of fabric and a little experimentation. These panels have infinite possibilities for design arrangements; keep the pieces in them medium-to-large in size, so that they are not too tiny to handle.

The Design

Start by drawing between six and eight 5cm (2in) squares on a sheet of paper. Then, using ruler and pencil, divide each square into between 10-15 shapes.

At this preliminary stage do not think too hard about creating a 'good design'. The important point is to get some designs down on paper from which you can select a suitable one. Try to vary the shapes and sizes for visual interest and avoid any shapes with a very narrow angle (less than 30°) as this may present problems in joining the pieces together.

The next step is to select a design that appeals to you from the ones you have drawn and draw it up to the actual size the block is to be. From 30cm to 40cm (12in to 16in) is a good size to start with. Number the pieces on your drawing in order of construction. Remember the rules established for the traditional blocks; it is easiest to start with the smaller shapes and work towards the larger ones.

Now make a full size tracing of your block design complete with numbers. This is your construction key.

Making the Pattern

Cut up your full size drawing accurately and stick each piece face up on to thin card. Then, using a quilter's quarter, add 6mm (¼in) seam allowance *all round* each piece and cut out. Mark the fabric grain on the pattern pieces by referring to the tracing.

Cutting Out

Place the numbered pattern pieces face down on the wrong side of the fabric, mark round the outside edges and cut out the shapes.

Assemble the pieces jig-saw style on a flat surface using the tracing as a guide. Stitch the block together using 6mm (¼in) allowances and pressing seams as you go — open if stitching on a sewing machine, to the darker side if sewing by hand.

Different effects can be achieved with the same block pattern by varying the fabrics used, or repeating the blocks in regular or random combinations.

These patterns can be used to make single block items, for example cushion covers, or they can be used in multiples to make larger panels for wall hangings or quilts.

POSSIBLE DESIGNS
Construct the blocks by joining smaller pieces together so that you can do as many long straight seams as possible.

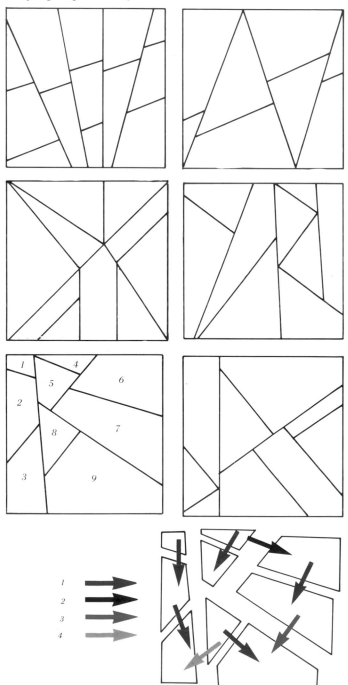

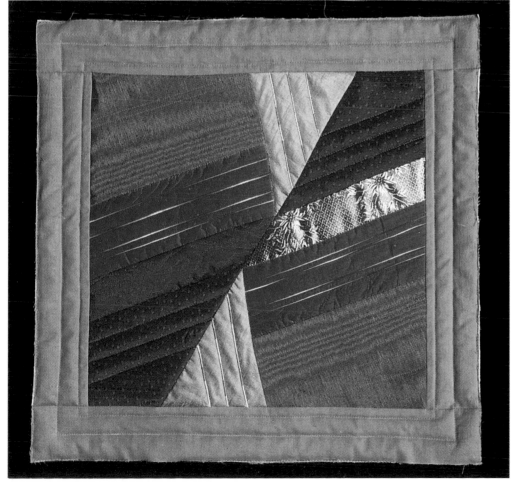

ABOVE AND LEFT Three of the infinite variations possible with this method of making abstract blocks.

CONTEMPORARY DESIGNS

LIGHT MAZE
The formal structure of a dark lattice dissolves into light at the centre of this
quilt. The contrast between light and dark, background and foreground is
emphasised by the fragmentation of the light centre, pinpoints of which are
carried to the edges of the quilt to shine through the dark grid.

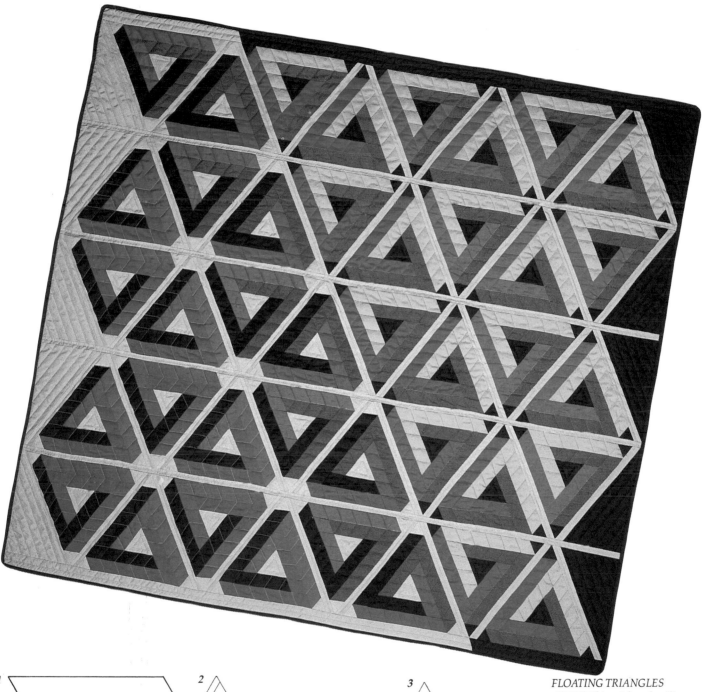

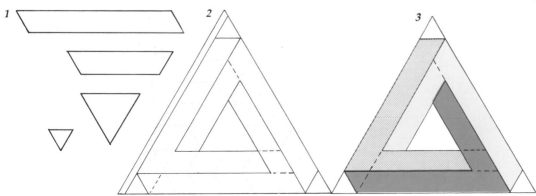

FLOATING TRIANGLES
ABOVE This patchwork quilt
presents a disconcerting 3-D effect,
produced by the careful positioning of
the light and dark fabrics.

PIECING THE TRIANGLES
LEFT
1 The templates needed for the basic
blocks.
2 Piece the triangles together as
shown.
3 Join the triangles with narrow
strips of pale fabric.

Chapter Three
APPLIQUÉ

INTRODUCTION TO APPLIQUÉ

Appliqué is the process of attaching cut-out fabric shapes to a foundation fabric by means of stitching, which may itself be plain or colourful and decorative. Essentially, appliqué is a two-dimensional technique which may be strictly functional, such as a knee patch on dungarees, or purely decorative such as a satin motif on a négligée. However, in picture making and more experimental work, it can be a vital art form in which personal statements are expressed. The play of light on surfaces, stitching, subtle modelling of fabric may all be exploited to create work with immensely tactile qualities.

The History of Appliqué

Early appliqué work which still survives includes pieces of applied leather from Ankmim, dated between the third and seventh centuries B.C., which decorated Egyptian coiffure supports. Geometric shapes were stitched with thread onto crescent-shaped pads to attach to the head.

Appliqué was used on the flags and banners of the Middle Ages which were carried into battle. Simple designs were applied to surcoats and jupons for the recognition of men wearing armour. At the start, only lords and knights carried devices, but later all their followers also wore heraldic symbols. It became a technical language of its own.

An era of remarkable English embroidery, known as *opus anglicanum,* developed during the thirteenth and fourteenth centuries, when professional workshops became world-famous for their magnificent embroideries. Gold and silver threads with silk embroidery on linen were applied to velvet backgrounds during this time. Ceremonial occasions, such as the setting up of guilds and livery companies, led to the making of civic, as well as religious, embroideries, and also palls used for the funerals of guild members. Separate motifs were worked with precious metal threads, coloured silks and sequins on a linen ground, applied and then neatly finished off with a twisted metal thread cord couched around the edges.

Sixteenth- and seventeenth-century appliqué was made for extensive use in the church and in great houses on bed valances and furniture coverings. As brocades and rich velvets became less costly and more plentiful, this type of embroidery declined. The availability of cheap cottons in the late eighteenth and early nineteenth centuries did, however, boost the use of appliqué for decorating quilts and coverlets, both in Britain and the United States.

An International Craft

Appliqué is an international embroidery form. Nineteenth-century Iranians used felted woollen cloth as a form of inlay. Shapes were applied edge to edge, with outlines of couched cords. This is known as Persian Resht work, the designs often resembling cloisonné enamel work.

Leather jackets with brightly coloured leather appliqué are a valued Hungarian tradition, as a protection against the cold. By contrast, in nineteenth-

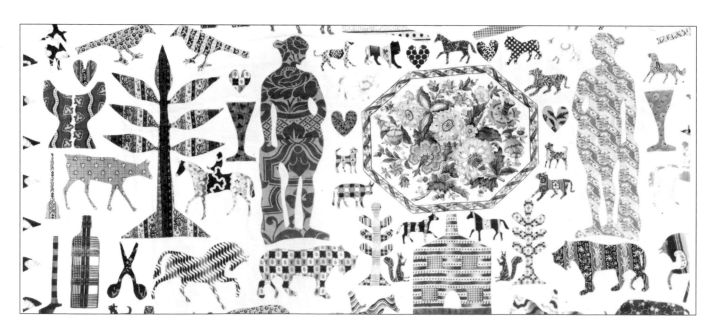

LEFT A cushion cover worked by Jessie Newberry in the early part of this century. Appliqué has been used in a typical art nouveau design, and the dominant colour throughout is a muted green.

OPPOSITE An appliquéd coverlet made in the 1850s and possibly intended as a marriage coverlet. The two female figures were probably inspired by Hiram Power's famous "Greek Slave" statue, shown in the Great Exhibition of 1851. The objects and animals, in wild profusion, have been cut from a variety of contemporary cotton prints.

century India, tents and hangings were made from cotton appliqué in bold designs, to provide shade while travelling. North American Indians devised a striking method of design for blankets and dress still used to this day.

In the San Blas atolls of Panama, and in northeast Colombia, the Cuna Indians work a traditional style of reverse appliqué known as "molas". The design, created by cutting linear shapes in step formation through several layers of different coloured, plain cotton material, reveals the pattern in reverse. The edges of each step are neatly tucked under and stitched.

Fabrics for Appliqué

Aside from its widespread use to decorate clothing and accessories, appliqué is often used today to create large and striking murals. The wide range of fabrics now available and the development of protective fabric sprays offer many advantages to the designer of hangings and panels incorporating appliqué.

Almost any material can be used in appliqué, and, like patchwork, a varied selection is often a stimulating source of design inspiration. Your ultimate choice should be governed by what you plan to make, bearing cleaning requirements in mind. For practical items, the fabric needs to be easy to handle and either washable or suitable for dry cleaning. While felt and lace scraps, for example, are excellent for picture-making, they would not wear well on a child's dungarees that have to be regularly laundered.

With delicate fabrics and those that fray easily, such as some silks and satins, a lightweight iron-on interfacing is recommended for extra support. Designs are transferred (in reverse) to the interfacing, either before or after ironing it to the wrong side of the fabric. The applied fabrics should not be heavier in weight than the ground fabric, although a second (finer) supportive layer can be added to the background, if needed.

One of the main features of appliqué is making fabric 'work' not just in colour and shape but in pattern and texture. Patterned fabric, for example, can be used to suggest all kinds of images and textures such as stripes for ploughed fields, flower sprigs for gardens, pile surfaces for animal fur and checks for brickwork.

DESIGNING YOUR APPLIQUÉ

It is essential to consider the purpose for the completed appliqué, and plan the design before beginning. Pencil several ideas roughly on paper. Simple, bold shapes are necessary for this type of embroidery. Tribal art is often simplified and a useful source. Outline shapes of leaves, petals, fruit and letters will initiate a free design, which can be added to as the work progresses. Compositions are more complex, and need detailed planning.

Consider the juxtaposition of colours in the intended design. Using colours next to one another in the spectrum, with small areas of opposing colour, may be a guideline. Also, light against dark colours, and warm against cold, can create interesting contrasts. Particular care must be taken for work to be used in a church or on a dark wall.

Drawing the Design

To plan the design, coloured paper cut into shapes, or designs or shapes taken from magazines, wallpaper or photographs, can be moved around until a pleasing arrangement is achieved. These shapes can be fitted with glue, tape or pins to a background sheet. It may be easier to create the whole design from one piece of wallpaper or from a picture. Either way, these designs can be transferred to the background fabric by using tracing paper, or by copying, preferably in sections.

LEFT The beautifully designed Monarchy embroidery worked by Audrey Walker in 1973, and displayed in the Pump Room at Bath. The piece is largely appliqué work, with additional embroidery for details and lettering. Most remarkable is the fashion in which the designer has contrived to make the different eras to flow into one another along the central pictorial section.

A more direct method of designing is to trace around templates onto the background fabric using a dressmaker's pencil or a hard lead pencil. Templates may be freely drawn, traced or copied onto a piece of stiff card and cut out, or they may be shapes cut straight from magazines or wallpaper.

If a shape is repeated in the whole design, it is sensible to have a paper shape cut from the template for each repeat, to maintain accuracy. Before cutting the pieces to be applied, it is important to match the grain of the background and the applied materials exactly, as the two materials then move together and will not pucker. (A pulled thread will define the directions of warp and weft threads in the fabric.) Some patterned materials, which demand a specific placement in the design, can be applied with iron-on interfacing. This can be used to prevent puckering, but will immediately change the character of the material. Test a scrap first, in case the iron-on interfacing alters the surface. You may also find that interfacing of this kind is useful for giving body to very fine fabrics, which might otherwise be unusable for appliqué.

Preparing the Fabrics

Felt and leather need no preparation before being applied but other appliqué fabrics may need to be backed with an interfacing to prevent fraying or to give extra body. Velvets and wools can also be backed with lightweight materials, and silks, cottons or linens with muslin.

Fine or lightweight fabrics may not need backing, but their edges can be turned under, ready for hemming to the article. First, mark the motif on the appliqué fabric. Cut 6mm (¼in) extra all round to allow for turning the edges under. Edges of curved outlines and corners may need to be clipped or notched so they can be turned under neatly. Finger-press the turned edges. It is best only to iron the edges if they are otherwise unmanageable, because this leaves a hem mark and destroys the slight puffiness of the two-dimensional edge.

For higher relief appliqué, the motif can be sewn down over varying thicknesses of interfacing templates, or can be stuffed with layers of wadding. You can also build the appliqué fabrics up, layer upon layer, to give the work a very tactile quality.

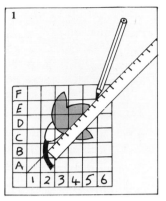

ENLARGING A DESIGN
1 Trace off the design and enclose it within a rectangle. Using numbers and letters to identify each section, divide the design into squares. (The more complicated the design, the smaller the squares should be.) Draw a diagonal line through the rectangle.

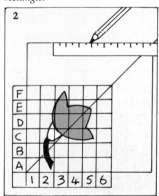

2 Place the design on the bottom left corner of a larger piece of paper and extend the diagonal line to the height needed. Complete the rectangle and divide it into the same number of squares.

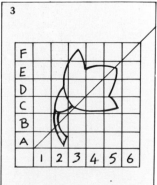

3 Identify the squares and draw in the design free hand, copying the lines from the smaller design.

USING TEMPLATES
Once you have decided on your design, you can use your original drawing to produce templates for cutting the fabric. Decide which pieces of your design need to be appliquéd first, and number the templates accordingly.

BASIC APPLIQUÉ TECHNIQUES

Stitching by Hand

There are several ways of stitching appliqué by hand, the choice depending mainly on the fabric used and the effect needed. Some methods are meant to be concealed, as in plain handstitching, while others are decorative, being embroidered or couched, or they can be both as part of the whole design concept.

On fabrics that fray, where turnings are recommended, secure the patches with slip hemming, or running stitch as shown here.

On non-fraying fabrics, such as felt and leather, cut patches without seam allowances and apply them unobtrusively with stab stitch or small running stitches, using a coloured thread to match the appliqué. The edges can, of course, be decorated afterwards.

Instead of tacking or pinning, which would make permanent holes, these materials can be held in place by applying a small amount of fabric adhesive.

PREPARING THE SHAPE

 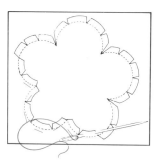

1 Mark the required shape on the fabric by drawing round a template. Remove the template and mark a second broken line 5mm (¼in) from the first.
2 Cut out the shape leaving another generous margin, about 1cm (½in). Only attempt simple shapes at first.

3 Work small running stitches by hand or machine just outside the innermost marked outline. These are stay stitches that will make the turning crisper.
4 Cut out the shape using the second marked line as the edge, and make cuts and notches along any curved sections to reduce bulkiness on turning under.

STITCHING METHOD A

1 Turn the edges under so that the stay stitching is just visible on the wrong side. Hold firmly and tack into place.
2 Place the shape on the background fabric and tack it lightly into position. Attach round the edge with neat slip stitch and unpick the tacking.

STITCHING METHOD B

1 Place the shape on the background fabric without having turned in the notched border. Tack the central area into position.
2 Slip stitch the shape into position, carefully turning in the border at the same time with the point of the needle. Stay stitching should not be visible.

STITCHES FOR APPLIQUÉ
*1 Running stitch. Take several
evenly spaced stitches on needle
before pulling through.*
*2 Slip hemming. Bring out needle
through seam fold of patch and take
a small stitch in ground fabric below.
Insert needle directly above, make
next stitch through fold and repeat.*
*3 Stab stitch. Bring needle through
just outside patch. Reinsert it above
close to edge and repeat.*

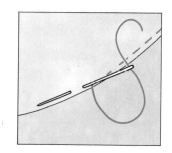 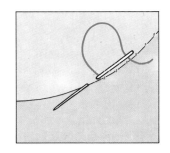 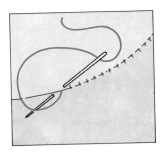

Stitching by Machine

Machine-sewn appliqué has the advantage of being hardwearing, most suitable for practical items, and generally time saving. This is also one of the areas in appliqué where new ideas can be quickly expressed. A combination of appliqué — superimposing different layers of fabric and printed motifs, for example — with free machining can produce unconventional effects. In experimental work, the contrast between raw edges, straight stitching, and the firm lines of zigzag and satin stitch offers a wide choice of linear expression. Braids, ribbons and strips of fabric can be applied by free machine techniques.

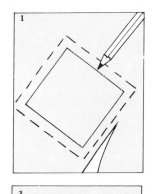  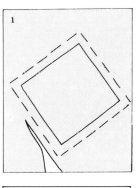 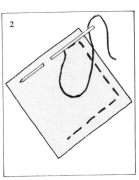

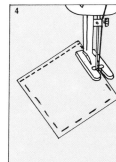 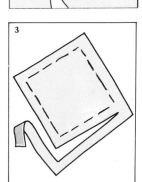 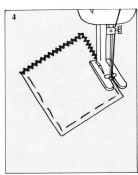

MACHINE STITCHING: STRAIGHT METHOD
*1 Pin template to right side of fabric and draw around the shape. Mark a second
line 6mm (¼in) outside this line, and cut out just beyond the outer line.*
*2 Staystitch just outside the motif line, and trim the patch on the outer cutting
line. Snip into curves and corners, fold turning allowance over to the wrong
side, and tack in place.*
3 Tack shape into place on backing fabric.
4 Machine round the edge with straight stitch. Remove tacking threads.

MACHINE STITCHING: ZIGZAG METHOD
*1 Pin template to right side of fabric and draw round the shape. Cut out leaving
1-2cm (½-¾in) extra fabric all round.*
2 Tack to backing fabric and straight stitch along the marked line.
3 Trim fabric back to just outside stitching line.
4 Work zigzag stitch over the edges of the shape. Remove tacking threads.

APPLIQUÉD MOTIFS

Motifs can be used singly or in groups, and working with a motif is probably the best way to begin appliqué work. You can use the motifs on virtually anything — clothes, bags, shoes, curtains, cushions, bed-linen, rugs, quilts, cot bumpers, soft toys. Once you are confident with a single motif, build up multiple ones or work with repeats.

The cardinal rule is to keep the shape simple; the more complex it is, the more difficult it will be to turn the edges under and appliqué the fabric successfully. For your first projects choose crisp cottons or cotton mixture fabrics that keep their shape easily, and use simple bold shapes. Appliquéing a plain motif to a patterned background fabric or vice versa is a simple but effective technique.

If your motif is going to be applied to a garment and will be washed frequently, wash the fabric first to make sure that the colours don't run and also to pre-shrink it.

USING FRAMES

NEATENING CURVES AND CORNERS

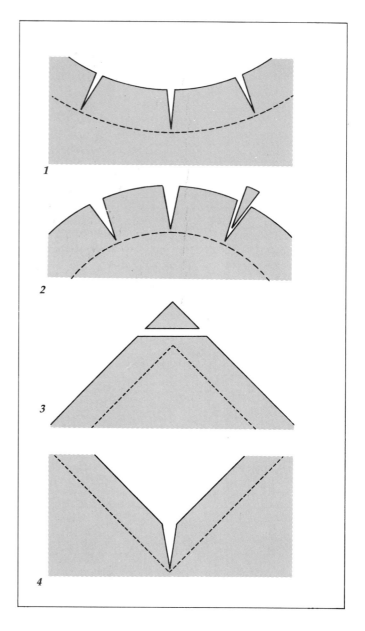

Where possible, stitching appliqué is much easier, and less likely to pucker, if it is worked in a frame. Small pieces can be stitched in a hoop and bigger pieces in the larger, rectangular slate embroidery frame.

The background fabric should be stretched evenly but not too tightly as the appliqué should be at the same tension. Hoops can also be used (upside down) with free machine appliqué, with or without engaging the presser foot.

Place the ground fabric over the inner ring, cover it with the outer ring and smooth out the fabric, stretching it firmly and evenly. Then, tighten the screw attachment. Tissue paper can be placed between the ring and the appliqué so as not to mark delicate work.

Seam allowances may vary from 6mm (¼in) to 2cm (¾in) depending on the type of fabric used and the purpose required. Straight seams can be neatened in several ways, but where a seam curves or where you need to eliminate excess bulk, the resulting seam allowance must be trimmed either by clipping or notching. This helps to give a really neat finish to your appliqué shapes.

1 On inner curves clip into the seam allowance as far as the stay stitching.
2 On outer curves cut out notches to prevent bulky folds forming underneath.
3 On outside corners trim the point back to reduce the amount of fabric in the mitred corner.
4 On inner corners clip into the point as far as the stay stitching.

*1 Templates for the tulip shapes.
2 Joining triangles for the border.
3 Opening out stitched triangles.
4 Making zigzags with two rows of triangles.*

ABOVE *This Pennsylvania German quilt made during the 1850s shows a typical tulip design appliquéd in bright contrast colours. Both figurative and floral motifs in fresh, primary colours are a traditional feature of Pennsylvania German design, and were used in their appliqué designs with great panache in various combinations of red, pink, yellow, green and purple.*

Here, the quilt, made from plain cotton fabrics throughout, uses appliquéd blocks — about 30cm (12in) square. These are pieced together in a square grid and finished with a zigzag border pieced from triangles of a colourful flower print and the white background fabric. The appliqué motifs are fairly large shapes with smooth outlines, which makes them relatively easy to work, and ideal for beginners. A single block — which might be a practice piece — is perfect for a cushion. Larger or smaller cushions can be made into all kinds of colourful sets with some stunning results. For example, a rainbow sequence could be introduced by reversing the pattern and using a dark background with lighter coloured motifs. Alternatively, six blocks could be used to make a crib cover in similar rainbow or pastel colours.

LACE AND RIBBON APPLIQUÉ

Some of the daintiest and some of the most striking effects in appliqué can be achieved by the same method — applying bought lengths of lace, ribbon, tape, binding etc onto background fabrics to create new textures. The designs can be as simple or ornate as you wish, but you'll find it best to practise on designs which have just a few layers of appliquéd materials.

If you are using slippery nylon ribbons, you may find it easiest to pin them to a backing board first while you weave them in and out and try different arrangements. You can then tack them together, remove them from the board, and do whatever stitching is necessary to hold the ribbons permanently.

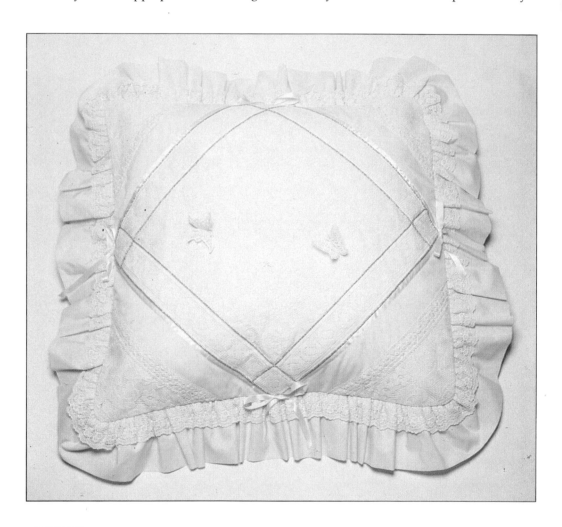

GARLAND
The design shows a large central diamond (with butterflies) and corner motifs cut from white cotton curtain lace and appliquéd on to a creamy cotton ground fabric. Straight-sided insertion lace is used to cover the edges of the motifs and the central border is further trimmed with gold piping and narrow satin ribbon tied in decorative bows. To complete the romantic effect, the pillow is surrounded by a deep double frill of cream cotton and scalloped lace.

Although designed to fit a large 60cm (24in) square pad, the appliqué design can easily be adapted to suit other shapes and sizes. A selection of mixed shapes combined with simple design variations would make a very attractive set of bedroom cushions.

As alternatives to lace curtaining, wedding lace, pieces of antique lace, filet net, edgings, doilies and crochet can be used for the appliqué with some stunning results. Other suitable ground fabrics include light- to medium-weight silk, satin, cotton and polyester.

CUBE

The sources of inspiration for contemporary appliqué design can differ widely. It may come from stained glass windows, aerial photographs of fields, primitive art, television graphics, or modern painting. Boldly drawn shapes simply outlined with a coloured tape or ribbon can make very striking images, as in this colourful abstract 'painting'.

Here, commercial tape (which requires no turning under) was used not only to cover the seams but also to provide an integral part of the design — using it as a line to link one unit to another — by being applied directly to the background. Such a technique makes this type of appliqué easy for beginners and fun to do.

Make a full-size drawing and stretch the background fabric in an embroidery frame, if preferred. Press on bonded interfacing to the appliqué fabrics, if needed, particularly on bigger shapes, flimsy fabrics or those that easily fray.

Cut out and position the patches on the background fabric, then pin and tack thoroughly to prevent them from slipping. Pin the tape or ribbon over the raw edges turning under the short ends or tucking them underneath adjacent edges. Machine stitch along both edges of the tape using matching coloured thread. Remove the tacking threads and mount your picture, as preferred.

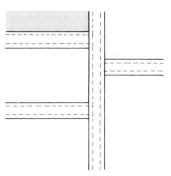

ABOVE There are several ways of applying the tape but the simplest is to tack and stitch in place all the horizontal pieces first, and then the vertical pieces on top, making sure they are accurately positioned, and all raw edges neatly covered.

PICTURE APPLIQUÉ

EVERYDAY LIFE

One of the best ways of producing whole scenes through needlework is to use picture appliqué. By using applied fabrics for the large areas you avoid the need to cover the background fabric with lots of repetitive embroidery, and you can choose fabrics which suit the subject by their texture and tone — flowered fabrics for curtains or gardens, for instance. Everyday scenes can be captured and immortalised by simple picture appliqué.

Stitching a Landscape

If you want to interpret a landscape in appliqué, one of the best ways to start is by making a sketch from a photograph. Draw in the main lines — don't bother at this stage with too much detail — and work out the order in which the main pieces will need to be applied. This usually involves beginning with large areas such as sky, hills, sea or foreground, then adding smaller details over the top.

ABOVE AND RIGHT Sea Bathing. The sketch shows the order of piecing the main fabric areas.

TOP LEFT Cherry Tree. Freely applied fragments of satin fabrics and lace together with stem, cretan and various straight stitches, have been worked onto a background, softly coloured with fabric crayons, to suggest the view of a cherry tree seen through a window. The whole picture is framed by an appliquéd window casement and roller blind.

LEFT The Country Wife, a three dimensional mural commissioned for the Festival of Britain, and designed by Constance Howard in 1951. The panel is worked to five-eighths life-size, and a wide variety of crafts and activities have been represented.

PICTURE APPLIQUÉ

SPECIAL OCCASIONS

Picture appliqué can be a wonderful way of recording special events — a baby's birth, a child's first day at school, a holiday, a wedding, an anniversary. You may want to represent the people involved, or make an appliqué picture of a house, or a room, or a landscape where something special happened.

You will probably find it easiest to work from a photograph, unless your drawing talents are especially good! Make a simple sketch of the main areas, then find fabrics which give the right kind of effect. You may want to include materials other than fabric, such as wood, wire, paper etc.

Cut and stitch the main areas of your design, following the general principle of stitching down the largest areas first. Then add secondary details, such as buildings and people, and finally put in the decorative details such as faces, furnishings, details on clothes etc. A variety of embroidery techniques can be used very effectively to add final detail to a picture.

ABOVE AND RIGHT Wedding Party. Much of the charm of this picture is its subject, which is quite realistically portrayed in a wide range of textured fabrics — all cleverly cut and embellished with embroidery stitches to show many fascinating and well-observed details. The sketch shows the order for piecing the main areas of the design.

SHADOW APPLIQUÉ

Shadow Appliqué uses sheer and semi-transparent fabrics overlapped on either the right or wrong side to give subtle changes of colour density. Combined with free machine stitching, and fabrics and threads rich in texture and colour, it offers wide scope for experiment. Gauze, organdie, lace, net, muslin, voile and other semi-transparent fabrics in mixed colours can be used for this form of shadow appliqué — a technique best suited to experimental picture-making. You may find silk organzas and other slippery sheers difficult to control whereas matt fabrics tend to 'stick' and are easier to handle in layers.

Make a full-scale drawing and indicate the colours before selecting the appropriate sheers. Choose a smooth cotton background fabric at the size required, allowing extra all round for stretching. Lightly transfer the main lines of the design to the backing, and then cut out the motifs by placing the sheet over the drawing and tracing around the shapes, allowing extra for fraying. Pin the shapes to the backing, starting with the background, then the foreground, and stitch in place before applying the details. Apply and stitch the bottom layers of the motifs before the top layers, trimming and fraying to finish; frame as required.

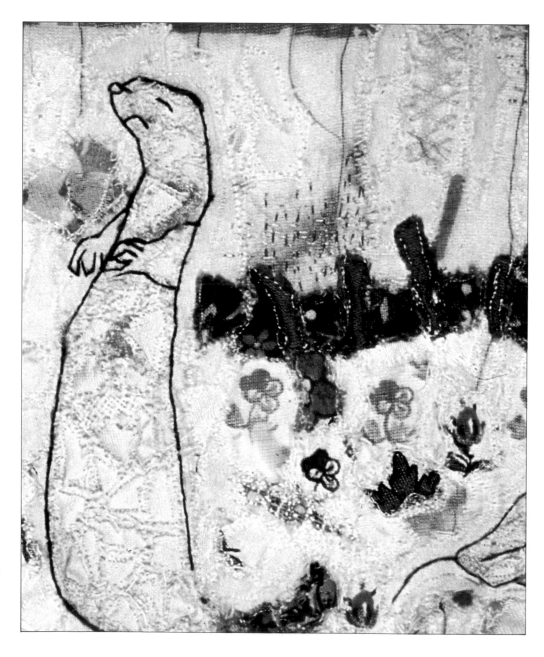

RIGHT Landscape with Otter. Fantasy appliqué is perhaps a more appropriate name for this technique, which uses only the tiniest pieces of fabrics and threads to express an idea so imaginatively, as in this landscape picture. The images, suggested in fabrics such as lace for the otter, cut-out printed flowers, and velvet foliage, are delicately outlined with colourful machine stitching. Light touches of fabric paint are added to the plain cotton background, overlaid in parts with sheer muslin which gives a soft, dreamy quality to the whole design.

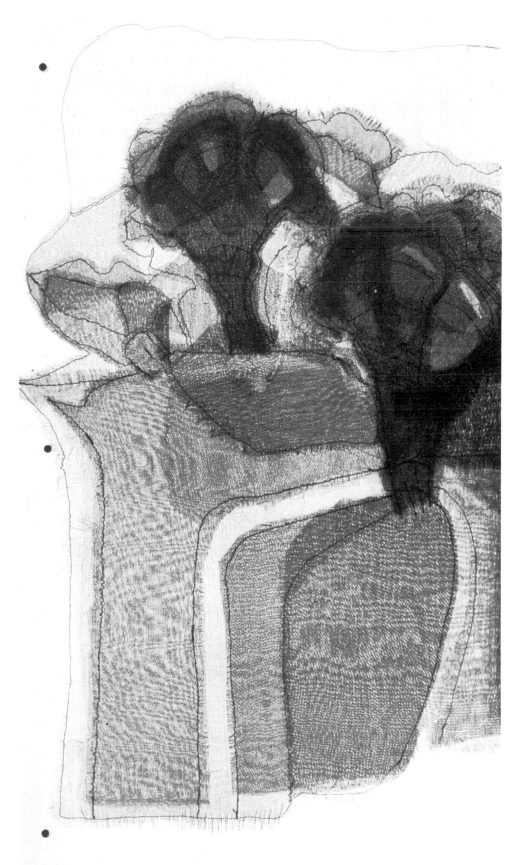

LEFT *Elm Tree Lane. In addition to the increased density of colour, overlapping gauzes produce fascinating watermark effects which lend a spontaneous quality to the whole picture.*

APPLIQUÉ PERSÉ

Appliqué Persé is the art of cutting shapes from printed fabric and appliquéing them to a background to form a new pattern. Small amounts of, perhaps, expensive or unusually printed fabrics can be skilfully arranged, thus maximising their effect.

Floral, rather than formal, motifs are much easier to build up into free-flowing designs, although stylised and geometric patterns can be included. These may be used quite graphically — perhaps as a patterned background or a flower vase, or as a trellis behind a trailing plant, for example.

Make a full-scale drawing, and select appropriate fabrics and cords. Cut the background fabric for each panel, the appliqué motifs and the borders, first backing them with iron-on interfacing, if needed. Apply the motifs, neatly oversewing them in place before couching over the raw edges and sewing the panels to the backing.

BELOW Salamander. The design uses several panels of heavy damask each bordered by one or more unusual prints. The appliqué motifs, cut from variously patterned and printed fabrics, are applied on top, and the main shapes outlined with couched braid or cord.

LEFT Flower Garden. Glazed chintz is used for both the appliqué and the ground fabric in both 'flower garden' cushion covers. These fabrics are excellent for repelling dust, but if you prefer to use an untreated furnishing fabric, then coat the finished cover with a silicone dust preventative spray — especially where light, pastel colours are used.

FOLDED APPLIQUÉ

This method of designing is popular in many countries including India, Pakistan, Hungary and Hawaii.

Designing appliqué with ordinary paper cut-outs is amazingly simple, and it was this technique that the women quiltmakers of Hawaii were first shown by American missionaries, which they quickly developed into their own individual style.

Interestingly, the small snowflake-type design taken by the missionaries soon grew in size to the proportions of the local vegetation which the islanders used as inspiration for their magnificent designs — the Breadfruit tree and the Pineapple being the most famous. These cut-out patterns, *kapa lau*, are often so enormous that they cover a full-size quilt. Other

favourite motifs, also taken from nature, include ferns, figs, paw paws, waterfalls and turtles.

Cutting the Patterns

Using two squares of different coloured fabrics (the lower one cut slightly bigger to include seam allowances), press and then fold the top layers first in half, then in quarters and finally in eighths. Pin the sections of the appliqué fabric together and transfer your design to the top section. Cut out very carefully and unfold. Position the design centrally on the ground fabric, matching the centre and diagonals. Pin and tack the appliqué in place, working from the middle out.

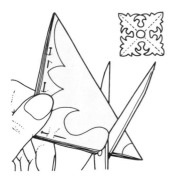

ABOVE *Holding the folded fabric firmly, cut out the design keeping the scissors at right angles to the fabric.*

RIGHT *This is a fine example of Meo hilltribe appliqué. Regular symmetrical patterns are made by first folding a square of fine cotton in half, folding in half again and then folding diagonally in half. On the final triangle a curved or linear design can be drawn and partly cut through — unfolded, the design will be an eighth-fold repeat. The square is tacked centrally to the ground fabric, the edges turned under with the point of the needle, and stitched to the base. Red patches have been inserted under the corners and in the centre. The tiny running stitches in the remaining spaces are worked from the back of the work. The yellow circles are worked in blanket stitch.*

LEFT This striking example of a folded quilt typifies the brilliant colour and bold, formalised design of Hawaiian appliqué. The design, which is intricately cut from cotton whole cloth using the folded technique, shows traditional motifs of Hawaiian flowers and foliage on a grand scale. The appliqué is first hand-stitched to a coloured background, interlined, and then quilted and the motifs outlined and filled with contour quilting so that the entire surface is covered.

ABOVE brightly coloured Hungarian leather jacket with red and brown leather folded appliqué. These jackets were warm and attractive, and very popular during the nineteenth century.

PADDED APPLIQUÉ

Beautiful relief surfaces can be made by padding certain areas or individual appliqué shapes. There are two very simple methods.

In the first, the appliqué is attached in the usual way, either by machine or hand sewing using slip hemming — this stitch giving a nicely rounded edge to the padding — but an opening is left in which loose wadding is inserted and the edge is then sewn down.

The other method uses a layer of wadding cut to the same size as the appliqué patch (less turning allowances) and the two layers applied as one.

Motifs in Relief

A more complicated way to pad appliqué shapes can provide amusement in a piece of work because the edges of motifs are not completely attached to the ground fabric — flowers and leaves, for example, treated in this way give a very pretty effect.

Pin two layers of appliqué fabric together with a layer of interfacing between to give body. Trace the motif on top, zigzag stitch around the outline and trim back the edges to the stitching. Make a small slit in the back and pad with loose wadding to give a pleasing shape. Over sew the slit. Position the motif on the ground fabric and secure either through the middle by hand or partially zigzag stitch to the ground fabric.

PADDED MOTIFS
Use a fine knitting needle to ease the wadding into the corners of a motif to give a nicely rounded surface.

RELIEF MOTIFS
After stitching around the shape, cut out the motif close to the stitching.

BELOW This contemporary quilt combines quilting and fabric dyeing with padded appliqué and embroidery.
The whole design is constructed like a 'nine-patch' block (as in patchwork). The central patch is a diamond-shaped flower-bed set between herbaceous borders with butterflies and flowers appliquéd in relief.

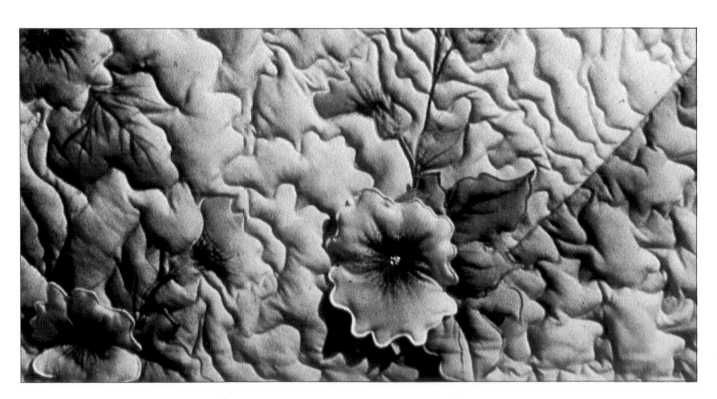

RIGHT *Rippling Stream. This spray-dyed and machine-quilted silk bag is cut out and quilted in one piece, finished around the edges with bias binding and decorated with padded appliqué flowers.*

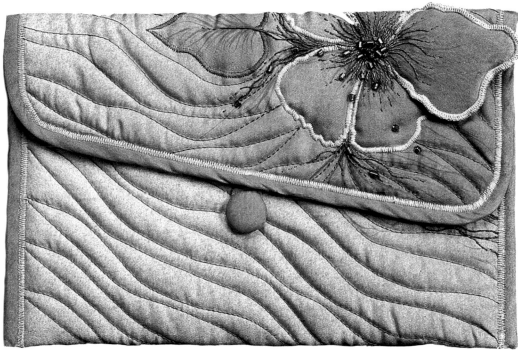

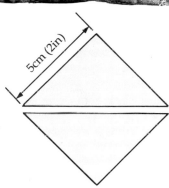

2 Flotsam template.

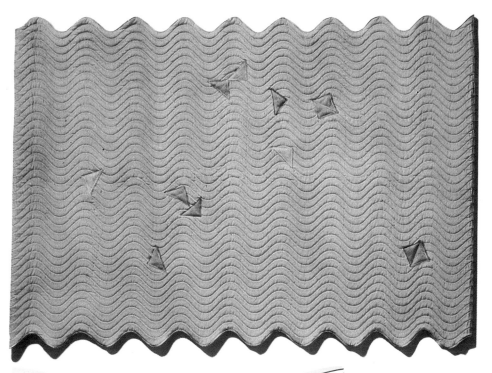

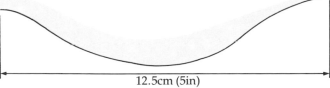

12.5cm (5in)

1 Wave template

Dancing Waves. A formal, symbolic water design is suggested by machining evenly-spaced wavy lines over the entire surface of this piece; fragments of fabric are appliquéd on top to suggest flotsam gently moving on the waves.

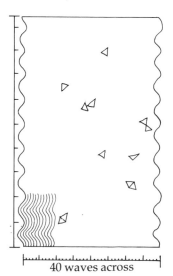

40 waves across

3 Plan of the quilt.

REVERSE APPLIQUÉ

The simplest method of reverse appliqué uses two layers of contrast coloured fabrics where shapes are cut away from the top fabric, allowing the colour beneath to show through. Other contrast patches can be sewn to the back as needed. This technique has been perfected by craftworkers in India, Pakistan, Thailand, Laos, and the Cuna Indians of Panama, who are famous for their distinctive designs.

The Cuna Indians have devised a more complicated method of working most colourful and intricate designs on their garments by applying coloured patches under second and third layers of fabric — even as many as six layers. The appliqué is worked in bright, primary-coloured cottons and the entire surface area is filled with the design, giving the finished work a well-padded, almost quilted effect.

BELOW A Mola blouse built up from a red panel with layers of fabric and coloured patches. The last layer of red is cut and sewn to produce frames, slits and cat shapes which have embroidered faces.

FIRST METHOD

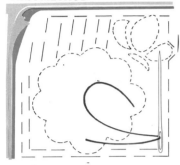

1 Place the selected fabrics on top of each other, align the edges if possible, and tack them all together. Mark the design on the top layer.

2 Cut out the pattern from the top layer of fabric leaving a margin of 6mm (¹/₄in) beyond the marked line for turning under. Do not cut the second layer inadvertantly.

3 Clip and notch the margin at curved sections and turn it under with the point of the needle back as far as the marked line. Sew edge to next layer neatly.

4 Continue to cut, tuck in and sew back each layer until the desired overall design has been realised. Work some stiches through all the layers if possible.

SECOND METHOD

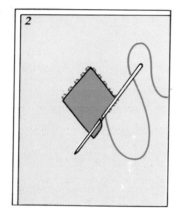

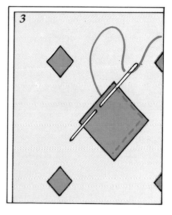

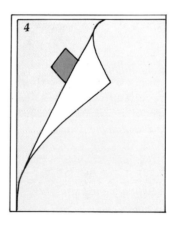

1 This design uses four different coloured fabrics.

2 With the ground fabric right side up, apply the four small diamond-shaped patches (with the edges turned under) and slip stitch them in place.

3 Working on the right side, apply larger diamond patches (with raw edges) in the centre and tack to secure. These raw edges will be covered by the next layer of fabric.

4 Position the second layer of fabric right side up over the appliqué and pin to hold.

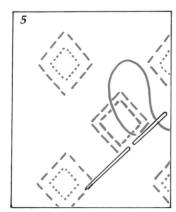

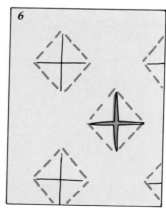

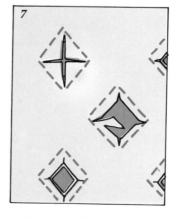

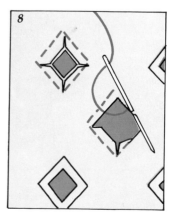

5 Turn the work over, and, with the wrong side facing, tack around the stitched areas, leaving a margin between of about 6mm (¹/₄in).

6 Turn the work right side up and snip into the corners as far as the tacking stitches.

7 Trim the excess fabric inside the diamonds leaving a fine seam allowance of about 3mm (¹/₈in).

8 Roll under edges and slip stitch. Leave tacking threads as a guideline.

RAISED WORK

As its name suggests, raised work is a three-dimensional version of appliqué. Many different cultures have developed their own versions of raised work, using padding, carved or stuffed shapes, layers of needlework and many other methods. Often the shapes are stitched and stuffed before they are finally applied to the background fabric in decorative designs.

Stumpwork

In the last three-quarters of the seventeenth century, a particular form of raised embroidery enjoyed a short period of prominence in England. This was commonly known by the descriptive term "stumpwork", probably derived from the French *estompé*, meaning "embossed". Stumpwork was characterised by three-dimensional doll-like figures, typically illustrating historical or Biblical themes. It was chiefly worked by the ladies of the great Stuart houses; often the finished embroideries were subsequently sent to be made up into cabinet or mirror frames by professional workmen. Some pieces were framed to stand as pictures on small portable easels. Others formed the panels on "caskets" or miniature chests.

Although stumpwork travelled to the North American continent with the establishment of colonies there, this type of embroidery, together with raised embroidery generally, went into a decline by the end of the seventeenth century. Later examples show these techniques taken to excess, which may have contributed to their fall from favour. Another factor in the disappearance of raised work was the arrival of Indian and Chinese goods and the resultant fashion for Chinoiserie. Today, many surviving examples have lost the colourful character they once undoubtedly possessed, but the dexterity of the work is still impressive and can only be fully appreciated if one tries to copy a piece. Modern embroiderers have adapted and used many of the techniques of raised work in murals and needlework pictures, often to vivid and striking effect.

ABOVE RIGHT *Young Edwardian Lady, a modern three-dimensional piece worked in 1974. This elegant piece demonstrates the adaptation of traditional raised work to contemporary designs. An almost ghostly effect has been achieved by working the figure's jacket in the same fabric as the picture's background.*

RIGHT *An example of the primitive raised work of the Peruvian Chimu, on which small three-dimensional figures have been depicted. It is a detail from a royal tunic in the form of a short shirt made from cotton and wool.*

ABOVE This piece of stumpwork, of outstanding quality and beauty, is a seventeenth-century Adam and Eve.

CONTEMPORARY APPLIQUÉ

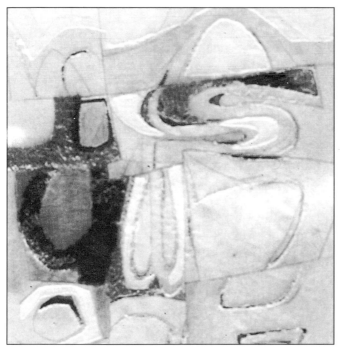

ABOVE Silver Jubilee Cope. Designed and worked by Beryl Dean, helped by members of the Stanhope Adult Education Institute, it is a remarkable piece of contemporary appliqué. The cope itself is made from a fine wool, and was worn for Queen Elizabeth's Silver Jubilee in 1977. It is now housed in the Treasury of St Paul's Cathedral.

LEFT A modern, machine-appliquéd panel 'Terracotta on white' contrasts the raw edges of plain calico on brown cotton with paint, crayon and hand stitches.

LEFT The Magic Garden designed and worked by Rebecca Crompton. It is an exuberant and original piece of work in which a variety of different techniques and stitches have been deployed. The Magic Garden was worked in 1937, and represented an exciting departure from existing designs and attitudes to needlework and appliqué.

CONTEMPORARY RAISED WORK

TOP Misfit is a piece of contemporary appliqué. After preliminary sketches were made of folded and draped material, the work evolved. A screenprinted background of dress patterns in sienna and orange complement the blue blouse with its foam-filled arm and leather hand. The latter holds a glass-headed pin.

BELOW This teapot sculpture made from quilted cotton and polyester filling and painted with acrylic shows the furthest limits of three-dimensional work: soft sculpture.

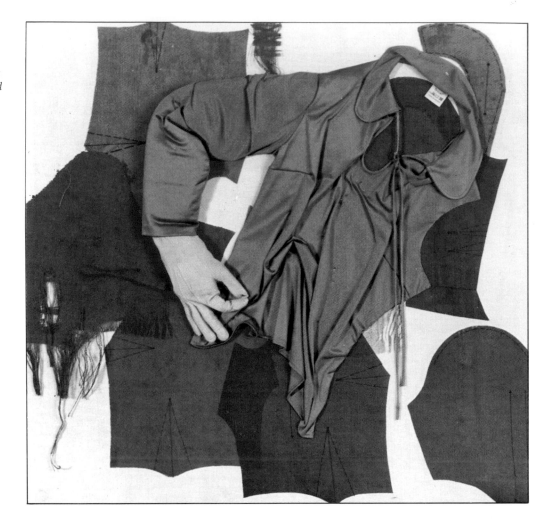

*ABOVE The Paget family; twentieth-century stumpwork worked between
1901 and 1927. The Paget family own a stumpwork
picture dated 1683, and worked by an ancestor Mary Ruddock who was
married to John Paget. This inspired Sir Richard Paget to draw and design a
picture of his family on the terrace at Cranmore Hall. The faces and hands were
carved in wax from which plaster casts were made and later painted. Each lady
of the family designed and embroidered her own costume and that of her
husband, child or brother. The magnificent foliage and family arms were
worked by Sir Richard's mother. Sir Richard Paget holds a stick of fused silica, a
newly developed process on which he was working at the time.*

Chapter Four
FINISHING TOUCHES

ADDING EMBROIDERY

Many patchwork and appliqué projects can be enchanced by adding surface embroidery to the design. There are many ways to do this, both formally and informally, and the choice of stitches, colours and threads make the possibilities endless!

TOP Bands of cross-stitch embroidery have been added to this patchwork tent-hanging from Afghanistan.

RIGHT Adam and Eve in the garden of Eden is the theme of this embroidered appliqué; hand-embroidery and machine-embroidery have been used with threads of many different colours.

ABOVE *Three different colours of threads have been used to outline the main shapes in this striking piece of appliqué worked by Henri van de Velde and his aunt at the end of the 19th century.*

LEFT *This lace appliqué cushion has been decorated with pink bullion-knot roses embroidered on each side and on the ribbons.*

MAKING UP QUILTS

Once you have produced several small patchwork or appliqué projects, you may well decide that you want to work on a larger project. A quilt is ideal, because generally you can work on the design in small units, whether you are working in patchwork or appliqué. It is worth making a fairly accurate design of how you intend the finished quilt to look, even if you are working in many different blocks and allowing the design to 'grow' as you work. Complex geometrical quilts need to be worked out very carefully so that you can be sure that you will stitch the pieces accurately.

RIGHT This coverlet was made in the 1850s by the friends of a woman called Mrs Waterbury. Different people worked on the different appliqué blocks, and many of the designs had religious or historical significance for the lady concerned; when all the blocks were complete they were assembled into a pleasing design.

ABOVE Quilts like the patchwork star here need very careful planning, though you can work on the individual star segments in small units. Careful thought has been given to the way the quilt pattern will be built up through different fabrics, quilted, and framed with a multiple border.

129

BORDERS

If you are making a large piece of patchwork or appliqué, especially if you are making a quilt or a wall-hanging, you will want to give some thought to the edge of the design, and whether a border would be appropriate. Borders give a neat finish to a design, and can act as a unifying element if you have used many different fabrics or colours in your work. They also give you another chance to show your creativity!

TOP The border around this Log Cabin Windows quilt has been formed from folded strips of the fabrics used in the quilt, producing an edging that tones in beautifully with the main design.

RIGHT The border on this quilt was pieced from flowered chintz fabrics, and is an unusual variation on the popular marriage of patchwork and quilting.

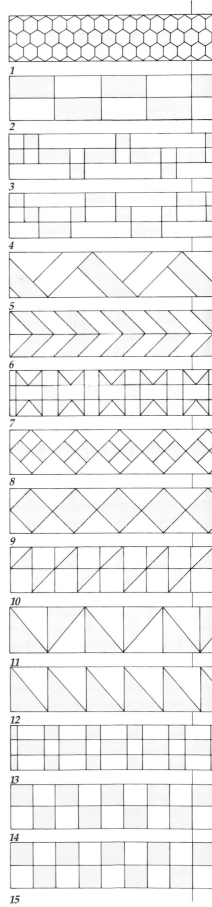

ABOVE The appliqué border of this quilt has been designed to complement the variety of pieced and appliquéd blocks in the centre of the quilt.

A selection of popular patchwork borders for quilts:

1 Rosette border;	**9** Sawtooth border;
2 Brick border;	**10** Arrow border;
3 Diamond border;	**11** Paris border;
4 Scallop border;	**12** Navajo border;
5 Hourglass border;	**13** Victory border;
6 Plains border;	**14** Target border;
7 Cascade border;	**15** Check border.
8 Zigzag border;	

BINDINGS

Once you have finished your patchwork or appliqué project, you will need to neaten the edges somehow. Conventional hems are possible, of course, but may not be practical if several layers of fabric have been stitched together; a binding may be a better choice, as you don't then have to turn under the edges of the stitched fabrics themselves. Bindings have another great advantage; they can be chosen so that they add to the pleasing appearance of your design as a whole. You may choose to pick out one of the fabrics that you have used in your patchwork or appliqué, or to make the binding in the fabric you have used for the background. If you are feeling extra adventurous, you can even make up a patchwork — or an appliquéd — binding so that it fully echoes the style of the rest of the project.

Once you have chosen the fabric or fabrics to use, you then need to decide which style of binding you will use. Straight bindings are easy for large, regular shapes like quilts, wall hangings and rugs, but if you have lots of curves to work round you could use a commercial bias binding or make your own from bias strips of fabric. Corners can be neatened in several different ways, and for extra sophistication you could add piping cord, either thick or fine, inside the binding fabric.

ATTACHING BINDING

This method gives a slightly padded binding as you are using a double thickness of fabric; it looks better than applying a single thickness to a thick piece of stitchery. Bias binding can also be applied the same way, or attached in a single layer in the conventional way; the binding can then be eased round corners in a continuous line.

1 Cut the binding 6cm (2½in) wide, and the length of the quilt edge.

2 Fold the binding in half along its length and press to firm up the crease.

Quilt right side

3 Pin and stitch the raw edges to the quilt on the right side. Stitch 6mm (¼in) from the edge.

4 Turn the folded edge of binding over to the wrong side of the quilt and hem it down.

STRAIGHT CORNERS

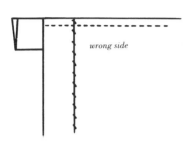

1 *Leave 1.5cm (¹/₂in) of binding beyond the second edge stitched onto the corner.*

2 *Turn the binding up and press.*

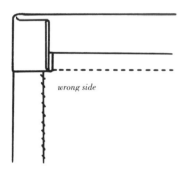

3 *Turn in the end and press in place.*

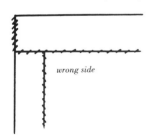

4 *Turn the binding over to the wrong side of the quilt and hem down.*

MITRED CORNERS

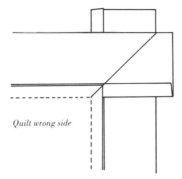

1 *Draw a straight line from the inner corner of the work at a 45° angle.*

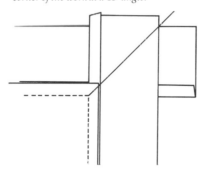

2 *Put the other edge of the binding to the top and repeat.*

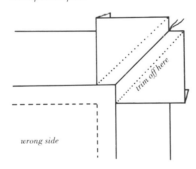

3 *Stitch the borders together along the marked lines and press open.*

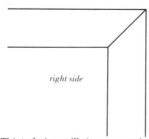

4 *This technique will give you a neat mitre at the corners of the work on the front; you will then need to turn under and stitch the raw edge.*

PIPING

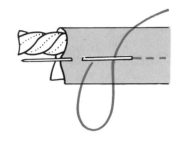

1 *Cut the required length of bias strip by the circumference of the cord plus 3cm (1¹/₄in) for seam allowances. Place the cord inside the strip right side outside, and stitch across close to the cord either by hand or machine using a piping foot.*

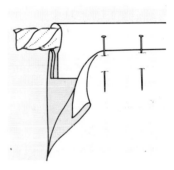

2 *For quilts, tack piping to quilt right sides together and raw edges even. Stitch close to previous stitching and press seams to the wrong side. Turn in edges of backing, pin over stitchline and slip stitch in place.*

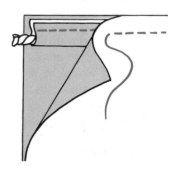

3 *For cushions, tack the piping in place with right sides and raw edges even. Ease piping around corners clipping into edge. Cover with second layer of fabric, tack and stitch through.*

QUILTING

PREPARATION

Quilting can often add the perfect finishing touch to a piece of patchwork or appliqué. The principle of quilting is very simple; the top layer of fabric is stitched to a backing layer, with an extra layer of soft material sandwiched in between; where the stitches are, an extra pattern appears on the work where the fabric is indented.

Quilting is a very practical technique when you want to build extra layers of warmth into the work you have done — for instance, if you are making a patchwork or appliqué bedcover or winter waistcoat. But it is also a very versatile decorative technique; the pattern of the stitching adds an extra dimension (literally!) to your work. It is particularly effective if you choose a quilting pattern that echoes the pattern you have used in your patchwork or appliqué.

Materials

The materials needed for quilting are very straightforward. As well as your project which you want to quilt, you will also need a piece of wadding the same size, and a piece of backing fabric. Wadding is available in various different thicknesses, and the thicker the wadding the more padded your final piece of work will be. You will also need a quilting needle, which is longer than an ordinary needle so that you can take quite a few stitches at once.

Tacking the layers together

If you are using a specific quilting pattern on your project, you will need to mark this on the fabric in tailor's chalk or dissolvable pen before you tack the layers together; once the wadding is in place the fabric tends to move out of position when you are marking patterns. The tacking is necessary so that the layers of fabric don't move in relation to each other while you are quilting.

Lay the backing wrong side up on a flat surface (on the floor if the quilt is large) and if possible tape it down. Smooth the wadding down gently on top, then the quilt top, being careful not to pull or stretch either as this may distort the quilt. Pin all three layers together, smoothing out wrinkles from the top and bottom. Starting from the centre, tack the three layers together easing excess fabric towards the edge. Cover the quilt with a grid of stitches 10-15cm (4-6in) apart.

ABOVE *A selection of different quilt fillers; top to bottom:*
1 *Different weights of polyester wadding (batting) are available; this is the 4oz weight.*
2, 3 *and* **4** *Silk in different weights.*
5 *Cotton Classic, a low-loft wadding.*
6 *Domette, a woven interlining suitable for wallhangings.*
7 *Needlepunch, a flatter polyester wadding.*

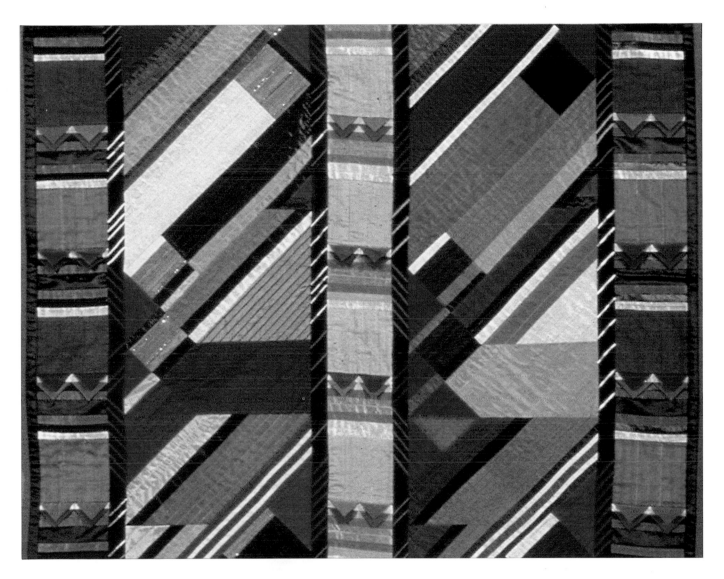

ABOVE This large hanging has been quilted very simply in straight lines that echo the lines of the fabric patches.

QUILTING

METHODS

There are various ways in which you can stitch the three layers of your quilted project together. You can tie the layers together at regular intervals with loops of thread (with or without letting the stitches show), or you can quilt in lines or patterns with rows of hand-stitching or machine-stitching.

Tie Quilting

For a quilt with a bulky filler such as 4oz or 6oz wadding (batting), or as a quick way to complete your quilt, tie quilting is ideal. Using thread in a strong natural fibre such as embroidery or crochet cotton, pull it through all three layers leaving an end long enough to tie — about 13cm (5in). Stitch again over the first stitch bringing the needle up near the loose end. Tie in a reef knot not too tightly as this might cause the fabric to tear. Trim the ends, or thread them into the quilt. Tie at regular intervals over the quilt surface, about 10-15cm (4-6in) apart. The knots can be used as decorative features either by themselves or in conjunction with buttons, beads or French knots.

Hand-Quilting

Hand-quilting is done with small, even running stitches through the three layers of the quilt. A close web of quilting was necessary on old quilts to prevent the raw wool or cotton filler from bunching together at one end of the quilt, but with the bonded quilt wadding available today you can do as much or as little quilting as you like. Close quilting is still admired for the added texture it gives.

To hand-quilt, take a 40cm (about 16in) length of single quilting thread and run it through beeswax, to strengthen the thread and help to prevent it knotting. Start with a knot and come up from the back of the quilt, tug the thread until the knot pops through the back. Try to keep stitches as even as possible; this is more important than their size.

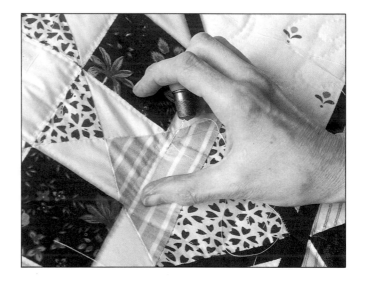

RIGHT Using a large quilting hoop; the close-up photograph shows the method of taking several stitches before the needle is pulled through.

Using Frames and Hoops

Quilting can be done on your lap, or you may prefer to use a hoop or frame. A quilting frame is a large and expensive item and if you have one you are probably already an experienced quilter. More accessible to the beginner is a hoop rather like an embroidery ring only larger — about 57cm (23in) in diameter. This may be on a stand, or can be rested against a table leaving both hands free. Keep the quilt fairly slack in the hoop and push the needle through from the top with a thimble worn on the middle finger of the sewing hand. Keep the other hand beneath the work to guide the needle back up. Expert quilters use a flat topped thimble on the lower hand, grazing the needle on the top angle as they stitch, which ensures that each stitch has gone through all three layers. Take three to four running stitches with a rocking movement, keeping the thumb pressed down on the fabric just ahead of the stitching. To finish, tie a knot close to the last stitch and pull this through between the layers, bring the needle out at the front and cut the thread off.

Quilting by Machine

If you plan to quilt by machine there are several points to consider. Tacking must be as thorough as for hand-quilting. Try to work out a quilting design which as far as possible runs in straight lines that do not cross. Turning a large quilt in the sewing machine is difficult; consider quilting larger items in two pieces and joining after quilting. To do this, when quilting is finished place the two halves right sides together and join through all thicknesses matching points where necessary. Trim away as much of the wadding as possible to reduce bulk, then pin a narrow strip of bias binding, matched to the backing, over the join and hem it to either side of the seam.

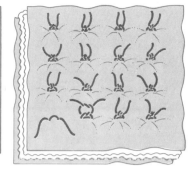
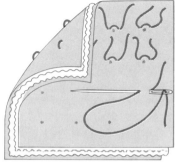

TIE QUILTING
1 Mark generously spaced dots onto the fabric as if for smocking, in the required pattern. Tack all the layers together.
2 Sew the thread or threads through all the layers at each dot. Leave one long end, work a backstitch with the other and tie off with knot or bow.

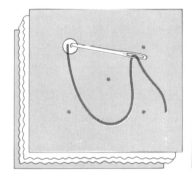
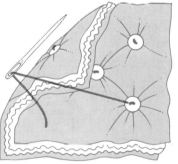

BUTTON QUILTING
1 Proceed initially as for tie quilting, but sew a button over each dot, with another placed precisely underneath it on the backing.
2 Secure the buttons firmly. They should sink down into the fabric. End off the thread amongst the central padding after every few buttons.

QUILTING AROUND PATCHWORK DESIGNS
1 In this Flower Basket design, the block has been quilted within the seam lines (known as sink stitching).
2 In the Paving Stones block, each shape is quilted along both sides of the seams.
3 The Jacob's Ladder pattern has been quilted diagonally through the patches to make a pattern which contrasts with the patchwork design.

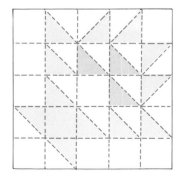
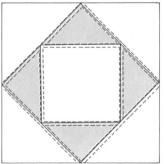
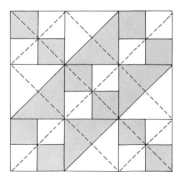

QUILTING

STITCHING PATTERNS

There are three main ways of approaching quilting patterns. First of all, you can use contour quilting, where you outline the shapes of your patchwork patches or appliqué motifs by stitching along or beside the seams (either by hand or machine). Secondly, you can draw a quilting pattern onto your fabric in specific shapes. For this method you can draw a pattern which echoes some of the shapes in your needlework, copy a pattern from elsewhere (perhaps picking out a flower pattern from one of your fabrics), or use a commercial stencil. Commercial stencils are available for motifs or borders, or all-over patterns, and range from the very simple to the very complex. The final way of quilting your work is simply to stitch in regular or random lines across it, by hand or machine.

ABOVE RIGHT On this piece of quilting the maker has stitched lines that suggest the patterns of water around the appliqué shapes of the birds.

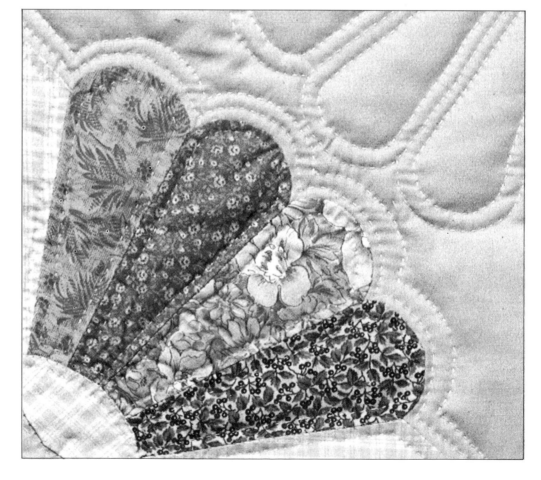

ABOVE On this Dresden Plate patchwork the patches have been outlined in contour quilting and echoed in a plain piece of quilting worked in a Dresden Plate design.

TOP Some of the many quilting patterns available commercially.

ABOVE A selection of border stencils for quilting. Sometimes border stencils also include corner blocks so that you can join border sections neatly at the corners of your work.

LEFT This basket-pattern coverlet has combined quilting with patchwork and appliqué blocks. The plain blocks and the border have been quilted in complex patterns, and the patchwork and appliqué baskets have been quilted around the fabric shapes.

DISPLAYING YOUR WORK

Once your patchwork or appliqué is finished, the final factor you need to consider is how you are going to display it. Wall-hangings are favourite ways of showing off work of this kind; you can stitch loops or casings into the top of the work or onto the back so that you can slip a rod through to hold the work straight, or you might prefer to have your project commercially framed if it isn't too big. Large hangings also make very good thick curtains, but if you have used several layers of fabric they won't gather very effectively, so will be best for straight curtains or ones attached at the top to wooden hoops. There are many other ways in which you can display your work, and you may want to put your projects to practical use too, as chair or bed 'throws', as cushions or cushion-covers, as rugs, cot quilts, garments or 3-D items such as workboxes, sag-bags or pincushions.

ABOVE A patchwork and appliqué chessboard makes a project that is both pretty and practical.

ABOVE This piece of strip patchwork has had casings added in the same fabrics as the patchwork so that a rod can be inserted.

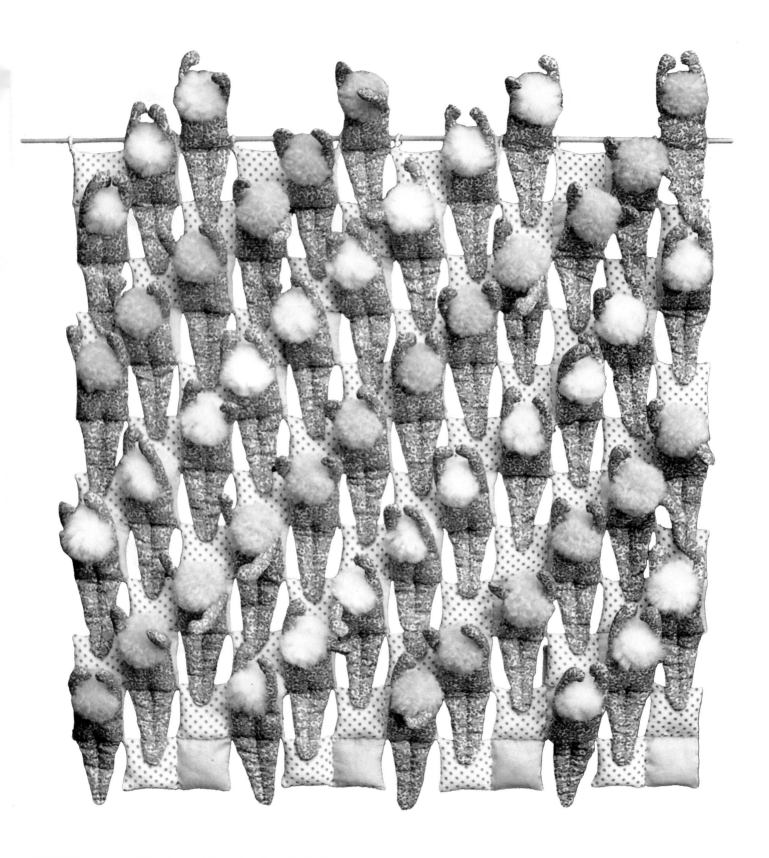

ABOVE This unusual wall-hanging, made in patchwork, appliqué and quilting, is called One Foot Square; a rod has been inserted through the final row of squares so that the work can be hung.

INDEX

PICTURE CREDITS

Key: t=top, b=bottom, l=left, r=right

American Museum in Britain, Bath: pages 6(b), 16, 21(b), 31(t), 33(b), 35(b), 46, 51(t), 67, 71(t), 92, 131(l), 139(b). Julie Athill: page 109. Bath City Council: page 96. Beamish, North of England Open Air Museum: page 130(b). Margaret Brandenburg: page 71(b). Moira Broadbent: page 83(b). Pauline Burbage: page 91(t). Victoria Bartlett: page 118(t), 122(b). Valerie Campbell-Harding: page 83(t). Cluny Museum, Paris: page 119. Christine Cooper: page 61(top), 140(r). Pam Dempster: page 28, 40-1, 60(l), 63, 64(l), 72. Denman College, Abingdon: page 104(b), 122(t). Eng Tow. Crafts Advisory Council: page 79(t), 80, 81. Ariella Green: page 105, 108, 126(b), Katherine Geurrier: page 22, 51(b), 75, 89 (all), 90, 124, 130(t), 135. Jean Gage: page 70(t). Dorothea Hall: page 36(l), 62(r). Diana Harrison: page 140(l). Herta Puls Collection: page 116. Francesca Kemble: page 58(b), Alison Kirby: page 44-45.

Kunstgewerbe Museum, Zurich: page 127(t). Beverley Marshall: page 24. Susan Maxwell, Crafts Advisory Council: page 110. Adele Outridge: page 127. Spike Powell, Elizabeth Whiting and Associates: page 68-69. Carole Proctor: page 85. Sue Rangeley, Crafts Council: page 7(t), 114(b), 115(t). Margaret Rivers: page 65. Glenys Sida: page 104(t), 107. Victoria and Albert Museum: page 94, 95, 118(b). Lesley Woodward: page 70(b), 126(t).

Every effort has been made to obtain copyright clearance for the projects featured in this book. Quintet Publishing would like to thank all the copyright holders who granted clearance, and at the same time apologies if any omissions have been made.

Thanks also to the following photographers: Ian Howes, John Coles, Charles Gage, Neil Woolford and Martin Gostelow.